Christus. Eloi, Eloi, lamma Sabacht...

Pharis. u. Voll. Sehet. Dem Elias ruft er...

Kaiphas. Lasset uns sehen, ob Elias kommt, ihn
herab zu nehmen? /: Der Vorhang des
Tempels zerreißt. :/

Christus. /: mit lauter Stimme :/ Der Hauptman sieht
zu ihm hinauf. /: Es ist vollbracht. —
Vater in Deine Hände empfehle ich
meinen Geist! /: neigt das Haupt :/
Erdbeben, alles zittert, und wankt. :/

Hauptman. Nach so heftigen Schmerzen, in den
Armen des Todes noch mit so lauter
Stimme reden können, muss dieß lä"ßt
was sonders an ihm ahnden. — Wahrhaft
er ist nur garnicht Man! er ist gottes
Sohn. — /: Erdbeben hört gehört :/

Aus der Fürstenfeldbrucker Handschrift von 1811.
Pater Dr. Othmar Weis

350 JAHRE
PASSIONSSPIELE
OBERAMMERGAU

Offizieller Bildband

Grundkonzept, Herausgabe und
Gestaltung

»Jubiläumspassionsspiele 1984«
Bühnengestaltung, Bildregie und
Szenenfolge

Text »Rückblick auf 350 Jahre«
und Text zu den »Lebenden Bildern«

Farbfotos aus den Jubiläums-
passionsspielen 1984

Übersetzung in die englische Sprache

Graphische Gestaltung und
technische Gesamtherstellung

Schwarz/Weiß-Aufnahmen
im Textteil

Printed in Germany
© im Eigenverlag 1984

Rechte

*Passionsspiele Oberammergau
1634–1984*

Gemeinde Oberammergau

*Spielleiter Hans Maier,
8103 Oberammergau*

*Pater Dr. Stephan Schaller OSB,
Kloster Ettal*

*Günter und Eva von Voithenberg,
8000 München (78)*

*Translingua Übersetzungsdienst,
5300 Bonn 1*

*Karl Thiemig AG,
8000 München 90*

*Ewald Haag, Oberammergau (15)
Günter und Eva von Voithenberg,
8000 München (8)*

*Gemeinde Oberammergau
– Gemeindliche Fremdenverkehrs-
einrichtungen –,
8103 Oberammergau*

RÜCKBLICK AUF 350 JAHRE | SURVEY OF 350 YEARS

Oberammergau stellt das Erlösungsleiden Christi in einer so monumentalen Weise vor, daß der gläubige Zuschauer eine religiöse Vertiefung erlebt und der skeptische Tourist der Ernsthaftigkeit der Darbietung seine Achtung kaum versagen kann. Gott hat es in der Fülle der Zeit gewagt, das Wort Fleisch werden und für uns leiden zu lassen. Dieses Wagnis Gottes ahmt Oberammergau immer wieder nach, wenn es Menschen die Rolle Christi übernehmen läßt, der unter uns wandelt, leidet, stirbt und zu neuem Leben ersteht. Woher dieser Mut, dieser Auftrag, dieses Spiel? Ein Rückblick tut not, gerade nach 350 Jahren.

Über geschichtliche Begebenheiten kann man auf zweierlei Weise berichten: wissenschaftlich oder überlieferungsgemäß. Jene Art wird einen Tatsachenbericht mit ehrlichen Lücken liefern, diese aber eine Ausweitung nach Art einer Legende. Bisher war man auf die etwa 1733 anonym niedergeschriebenen *»Merkwürdigen Begebenheiten«* aus der Dorfgeschichte (seit 1574) angewiesen, kurz CHRONIK genannt; wir können sie nicht mehr überprüfen, da sie am Ende des 19. Jahrhunderts verlorenging. Jedenfalls lag sie noch dem Pfarrer ALOIS DAISEN-BERGER vor, als er anno 1858 die *»Geschichte des Dorfes Oberammergau«* schrieb, desgleichen seinem Amtsbruder JOHANN BAPTIST PRECHTL von Unterammergau, als er sich 1859 mit einer kritischen Arbeit über Oberammergau in Erlangen den philosophischen Doktorgrad erwarb. Schon letzterer hat betont, daß die Aufzeichnungen jener CHRONIK *»wohl der Hauptsache nach richtig sind, im Einzelnen aber der Berichtigung bedürfen«.* Wäre Oberammergau nicht so weltberühmt geworden, könnte man dies auf sich beruhen lassen; jetzt aber, da es sein 350jähriges Jubiläum feiert, andererseits aber auch kritische Stimmen behaupten, es könne frühestens 1644 gespielt haben, müssen Beweise für das erste Spiel im Jahre 1634 erbracht werden. Man möge es dem Verfasser dieses Berichtes nicht verübeln, wenn er erstmals der bisher allein maßgebenden CHRONIK mißtraut und sich lieber auf archivalische Quellen stützt, diese aber in den geistigen und kulturgeschichtlichen Verhältnissen jener frühen Zeiten beläßt. Ein Glück, daß auch gerade aus der naheliegenden Benediktinerabtei Ettal noch einige Aktenbestände zur Verfügung stehen, die bisher nicht ausgewertet worden sind!

Oberammergau presents Christ's redemptive suffering in such a monumental way that the devout spectator experiences deep religious involvement and the sceptical tourist cannot refuse to pay respect to the seriousness of what he is shown. In the fullness of time God dared to let the Word become flesh and to suffer for us. Time after time this venture by God is followed by Oberammergau when it allows men to take the role of the Christ who walks among us, suffers, dies and rises again to new life. Where does this courage, this mission, this play come from? A survey is needed, especially after 350 years. Historical events can be related in two ways: scientifically or according to tradition. The former method will provide a factual report with honest gaps, but the latter will give an expanded account in the manner of a legend. Previously we have had to rely on the *"Remarkable Events"* from the history of the village (since 1574), called "CHRONICLE" for short, written by an anonymous hand about 1733; this can no longer be examined because it was lost at the end of the 19th century. At any rate it was still available to the priest ALOIS DAISENBERGER when he wrote the *"History of the Village of Oberammergau"* in 1858, and also to his brother minister JOHANN BAPTIST PRECHTL of Unterammergau, when he took the degree of Doctor of Philosophy in Erlangen with a critical work on Oberammergau in 1859. Even the latter emphasised that the writings in the CHRONICLE *"are no doubt mainly correct, but require correction in details".* If Oberammergau had not become so famous throughout the world, the matter could have been left there. But now that it is celebrating its 350th Jubilee while on the other hand critical voices allege that the play could have been given at the earliest in 1644, proof must be furnished for the first play in 1634. The writer of this report should not be blamed if he is the first to mistrust the CHRONICLE, which has hitherto been the only authoritative source, and prefers to rely on archive sources while placing them in the spiritual and historical context of those early times. It is fortunate that there are still some collections of documents of the Benedictine Abbey of Ettal which have not yet been examined.

DIE PEST IN OBERAMMERGAU

Oberammergau war ein dem bayerischen Stamm der Huosi angehöriges Dorf. Aufgrund der dort wie in anderen Orten der Umgebung gefundenen merowingischen Reihengräber (7. und 8. Jahrhundert) war es schon alt, als es im Jahre 1330 von Kaiser Ludwig IV., meist *»dem Bayern«* genannt, dem von ihm infolge eines Heimkehrergelübdes gestifteten Benediktinerkloster Ettal nebst anderen Gütern geschenkt wurde. Die vier *»Hofmäder«* Oberammergau, Unterammergau, Kohlgrub und Soyen (heute Bayersoien) bildeten eines von den *»Stiften«*, mit denen das Kloster damals ausgestattet wurde. Zur Grundherrschaft gehörte die niedere Gerichtsbarkeit, im Ettaler Falle jedoch auch die hohe Gerichtsbarkeit, da dem Kloster zugleich das *kayserlich gefreite Pfleggericht* in Murnau übertragen war. Keines der Ettaler Dörfer hatte einen Schultheiß oder sonstwie genannten Vorsteher, sondern es hatte nach altem Herkommen eine kollegiale Selbstverwaltung, die aus den von den männlichen Gemeindemitgliedern gewählten *»Söchs«*, d. h. 6 Gemeinderäten, bestand, deren Wahl der Abt von Ettal genehmigen mußte. Letzterem wurden über seinen in Oberammergau seßhaften Richter alljährlich die Gemeinderechnungen vorgelegt; die *»Söchs«* hatten entsprechende *Verbescheidungen* entgegenzunehmen. Nur bei außerordentlichen Ausgaben mußten sie den Abt vorher um Erlaubnis bitten. Außerdem wurde von der Gemeinde noch ein Rat von 12 Männern gewählt, der aber mehr repräsentative Pflichten hatte. Im übrigen konnten sich die *»Söchs«* beim Abt über den Richter beschweren und beim Herzog in München über den Abt und seinen Pfleger in Murnau, wovon zur Freude des Historikers besonders ausgiebig Gebrauch gemacht wurde.

Passionsbühne (1820)

THE PLAGUE IN OBERAMMERGAU

Oberammergau was a village belonging to the Bavarian tribe of the Huosi. On the evidence of the rows of Merovingian graves dating from the 7th and 8th centuries which have been found there and in other places in the neighbourhood, Oberammergau was already old when it was given in 1330, together with other estates, by the Emperor Ludwig IV, usually called *"the Bavarian"*, to the Benedictine monastery of Ettal which he had founded in fulfilment of a vow made on his homecoming. The four *"Hofmäder"* of Oberammergau, Unterammergau, Kohlgrub and Soyen (now Bayersoien) constituted one of the *"foundations"* with which the monastery was then endowed. Rule over the land entailed responsibility for the inferior courts of law and, in the case of Ettal, the superior courts also because the district court, which had been freed by the Emperor, in Murnau was transferred to the monastery at the same time. None of the Ettal villages had a mayor or any other kind of overseer, but in accordance with the old custom they had a self-governing body consisting of the *"Söchs"*, i.e. six parish councillors elected by the male members of the parish, but whose election had to be approved by the Abbot of Ettal. The parish accounts were submitted to the Abbot each year through his resident judge in Oberammergau; the *"Söchs"* had to receive the corresponding approvals or objections. They had to ask the Abbot for prior consent only for exceptional expenditure. In addition the parish elected a council of twelve men which however performed more representative duties. Furthermore the *"Söchs"* could complain to the Abbot about the judge and to the Duke in Munich about the Abbot and his curator in Murnau. To the

Eine ständige Quelle des Ärgers waren die Waldrechte. Einerseits gehörte der Wald zur Stiftungsausstattung des Klosters, andererseits hatte er auch dem Bedarf der Gemeinden zu dienen (Heizung, Hausbau, Dachschindeln, Hausrat, Viehgatter, Werkzeuge, Schnitzereien). Ettal hatte kurzerhand zwei Drittel seines Waldbestandes den Dörfern überlassen und sich das nur wenig besiedelte Graswangtal vorbehalten, wo die Fichten vor allem an den schattigen Nordhängen der Berge zwar langsamer, aber dafür gerader und fester wuchsen; heute noch heißt ein Waldteil »Schattenwald«. Gerade solches Holz benötigte man für eine große Bühne im Freien. In Oberammergau war schon 1330 aller Grund und Boden vergeben, weshalb es keinen eigenen Dorfplatz besaß, sondern nur einen größeren Friedhof, in dessen nördlicher Ecke eine kleine Kirche aus gotischer Zeit stand. Man lebte vorwiegend von der kargen Landwirtschaft, zum Teil zusätzlich vom Vertrieb von Schnitzwaren und von der Güterbeförderung (Rottwesen) auf dem Straßenstück Partenkirchen–Schongau. Aber gerade diese Durchgangsstraße brachte auch Unheil ins Dorf.

Am 4. 6. 1632 waren auf ihr schwedische Reiter bis Ettal vorgedrungen, hatten dort einen jungen Pater und den Organisten niedergemacht und auch in Oberammergau Spuren gewaltsamen Einbruchs hinterlassen. Weitere Überfälle verhinderte der kaiserliche Generalissimus WALLENSTEIN, indem er bei Fürth eine strategisch sehr wohlbedachte Sperrstellung einnahm und die Schweden zwang, sie erfolglos zu bestürmen und ihm in einem mühsamen Abnützungskrieg zu ihren nördlichen Glaubens- und Bundesgenossen zu folgen, wo König Gustav Adolf dann in der Schlacht von Lützen am 16. Nov. 1632 fiel. Bayern war frei, aber der Krieg hatte einen zwar unsichtbaren, aber tödlichen Feind hinterlassen: die PEST. Nicht zum ersten Male wanderte der »Schwarze Tod« durch Europa. Man kannte den Erreger nicht (erst 1894 wurde er entdeckt), wußte aber, daß er sich durch Ratten (besonders auf Schiffen) und Ungeziefer verbreitete und sich schließlich auch an Vieh und Menschen wagte. Wenn auch nicht jede Pestbeule, die der Körper zur Abwehr der Eindringlinge im Lymphsystem bildete, zum Tode führte, so war doch keine Rettung mehr möglich, sobald die Lunge erfaßt war. Viele riegelten sich ab oder entflohen; grundsätzlich näherte man sich nur auf Rufweite. In den Jahren 1634 und 1635 soll die Pest in München allein fast 15 000 Opfer unter der Bevölkerung gefordert haben. Von dem Nachbardorf *Kohlgrub*

historian's joy, extensive use was made of this right.

Forest rights were a constant source of vexation. On the one hand the forest belonged to the endowment of the monastery, on the other it also had to serve the needs of the parishes (heating, building, roof shingles, household equipment, cattle fences, tools, wood carvings). Ettal had at once given two thirds of its forests to the villagers and kept for itself only the thinly populated Graswang valley, where the fir trees mainly on the shaded northern slopes of the mountains grew more slowly but straighter and stronger; part of the forest is still called *"Schattenwald"* today. Timber of precisely this kind was needed for a large open-air stage.

As early as 1330 all land in Oberammergau had been distributed, so that it did not have a proper village square but only a large graveyard in the northern corner of which stood a small Gothic church. Most people gained a meagre living from agriculture, some of them also selling wood carvings and working as carriers on the section of highway from Partenkirchen to Schongau. However, it was also this thoroughfare which brought one more time disaster to the village.

On 4th June 1632 Swedish horsemen advanced along the road as far as Ettal, where they killed a young priest and the organist, also leaving traces of forcible housebreaking in Oberammergau. Further raids were prevented by the Emperor's general, WALLENSTEIN, who took up a strategically well-planned blockade position near Fürth, compelling the Swedes to storm it unsuccessfully and to follow him in a strenuous war of attrition to their northern allies of the same faith, where King Gustav Adolf fell in the battle of Lützen on 16th November 1632. Bavaria was free but the war had left behind an invisible, but deadly enemy: the PLAGUE. It was not the first time the *"Black Death"* passed through Europe. The causative agent was not known (it was only discovered in 1894), but it was known to be spread by rats (especially on ships) and vermin, finally venturing to attack cattle and humans. Although not every plague spot which the body developed to repulse the intruders in the lymphatic system led to death, salvation was impossible once the lungs were attacked. Many people locked themselves indoors or fled; in principle no-one came closer than calling distance. In 1634 and 1635 the plague is said to have claimed almost 15,000 victims amongst the people in Munich alone.

Concerning the neighbouring village Kohlgrub the CHRONICLE reported: *"In the parish of Kohlgrub so*

Totenbuch Oberammergau (1632–1633)

berichtete die CHRONIK: »*In der Pfarre Kohlgrub sind die Leute dermaßen ausgestorben, daß nur 2 Paar Ehefolk anzutreffen gewesen, eines Theils aus einem Hauß ist der Mann oder das Weib gestorben, etliche Häuser gar ausgestorben.*« Das war nachprüfbar. Leider setzen die Sterbelisten in Kohlgrub erst 1669 ein, aber die alten Taufregister sind erhalten, die einen jährlichen Durchschnitt von 30 Geburten aufweisen, 1632 sogar 50, 1633 immerhin 29, 1634 wieder 37. Es scheint, daß die CHRONIK doch stark übertrieben hat. Eine echte Überraschung bereiten uns jedoch die Hochzeitslisten. Während 1633 noch 6 Hochzeiten notiert sind, sind es 1634 tatsächlich nur 2 (wohl die Quelle für die Behauptung in der CHRONIK). Im Jahre 1635 sind hingegen nicht weniger als 39 Paare an den Altar getreten – ein wahrer Hochzeitsboom; wenn wir sie genauer anschauen, finden wir darunter 10 Witwer, 16 Witwen und 8 hinterbliebene Töchter. Das sehr schwer heimgesuchte Kohlgrub lebte wieder auf und baute 1637 sogar die dem Pestpatron St. Rochus gelobte Kapelle, die noch heute die Mär von den zwei Paar Ehevolk poetisch in Erinnerung wachhält.

Wie steht nun Oberammergau vor diesem so düsteren Hintergrund? Glücklicherweise haben sich aus jenen bösen Jahren vier Register erhalten, die gegen Ende des 17. Jahrhunderts in einem Pergamentumschlag zusammengeheftet worden sind. Sie befinden sich im Besitz der Pfarrei, jedoch ist nur ein einziges davon pfarramtlich, d. h. vom jeweiligen Pfarrer, der Angehöriger des nahen Augustinerstiftes Rottenbuch war, selbst geführt: das Taufregister, vom Pfarrer JOHANNES GASTL 1613 begonnen und bis 1623 geführt, dann von seinen Nachfolgern weitergeführt, die gelegentlich ihre Namen nennen. Die anderen Register hat VALENTIN PAUHOFER angelegt, der anscheinend Organist und Chorleiter und somit auf Einkünfte aus dem Kirchendienst angewiesen war. 1619 begann er ein Schuldenregister, worin er alle Schuldner notierte, dazu auch die »*Freundschaften*«, die bei einem Begräbnis oder Jahrtag zum Opfergang gebeten wurden oder deren gedacht wurde. Da bei diesen »*Freundschaften*« auch Äbte und Mönche von Ettal inbegriffen waren, die aus den Klosterakten datierbar sind, erhalten wir Jahreszahlen wie 1549, 1566, 1590, 1615, 1617, 1625, 1626. 1618 begann PAUHOFER ein zweites einträgliches Register, das der Hochzeiten, denn zu jeder Hochzeit gehörte Musik. Schließlich folgt sein für uns wichtigstes Register: »*Verzaichnus der gestorbenen persohnen, welche alhir zu Ober-Ammer-*

many people died that only two married couples could be found, in some cases the husband or the wife of the house died, several houses died out completely." This could be proved. Unfortunately the registers of deaths in Kohlgrub begin only in 1669, but the old registers of baptisms have been kept which show an annual average of 30 births, with as many as 50 in 1632, still 29 in 1633 and 37 again in 1634. It appears that the CHRONICLE exaggerated considerably. However, the marriage registers have a real surprise for us. While six marriages are recorded for 1633, there are indeed only two for 1634 (no doubt the source for the statement in the CHRONICLE). By contrast, in 1635 no fewer than 39 couples went to the altar – a real marriage boom; if we consider them more closely, we find among them 10 widowers, 16 widows and 8 surviving daughters. After its severe affliction, Kohlgrub returned to life and in 1637 even built a chapel dedicated to St. Rochus, the patron saint of the plague. The chapel poetically keeps alive the story of the two married couples even today.

What of Oberammergau, against this sombre background? Fortunately four registers have been preserved from those black years, stitched together in a parchment cover towards the end of the seventeenth century. They are in the possession of the parish, but only one of them, the register of baptisms, was kept officially, i.e. by the parish priest, who belonged to the nearby Augustinian monastery of Rottenbuch. This register was begun by the parish priest JOHANNES GASTL in 1613 and kept by him until 1623, then continued by his successors who sometimes give their names. All the other registers were started by VALENTIN PAUHOFER, who was evidently an organist and choirmaster and therefore relied on income from church services. In 1619 he began a register of debts in which he noted every debtor, and also the "kindred" who were invited to the offertory at a burial or who were remembered at an anniversary. Since these "kindred" also included abbots and monks of Ettal who can be dated from the monastery records, we obtain dates such as 1549, 1566, 1590, 1615, 1617, 1625 and 1626. In 1618 PAUHOFER began a second lucrative register, the register of marriages, because music was a part of every wedding. Lastly comes his register which is most important for us: *"List of deceased persons who have passed away in God each year here in Ober-Ammergau, as follows 1621."* Normally death took only one inhabitant of Oberammergau a month, sometimes two,

1. Passionsspiel 1634 (Rekonstruktion von Mettenleitner)

gau jedes Jar in Gott verschiden seind, wie volgt 1621.« Für gewöhnlich hat der Tod monatlich nur einen Oberammergauer geholt, mitunter zwei, mitunter keinen. Es mußte auffallen und beunruhigen, daß Ende November 1632 die Sterbezahl zu steigen begann, wie nachstehendes Schaubild zeigt:

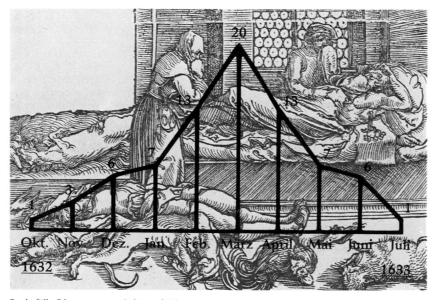

Sterbefälle Oberammergau (1632–1633)

Auch ein medizinisch nicht geschultes Auge sieht sofort, daß hier eine ansteckende Krankheit ausgebrochen ist, die im März 1633 ihren Höhepunkt und im Juli bereits ihr Ende erreichte. Da diese aktenmäßige Totenliste nicht mit den Angaben der CHRONIK in Einklang zu bringen ist, hat man sie in Mißkredit zu bringen gesucht, als ob die

überlasteten Pfarrer beim Eintragen der Sterbefälle nachlässig gewesen wären; dabei haben die Pfarrer überhaupt keine eingetragen. Übrigens benützen pfarramtliche Eintragungen (z. B. Taufen, die ohne Musik erfolgten) immer die korrekten Heiligennamen aus dem Römischen Meßbuch, alle anderen die

Umgangsnamen, z. B. Apelania (Apollonia), Duredea (Dorothea), Mathoyß (Matthias) usw. Dabei wissen wir nicht einmal, ob alle eingetragenen Namen auch Pestopfer waren; die Taufliste kennt jedenfalls keine frühgestorbenen Kinder. Sehr selten finden sich Zusätze, die uns einen kleinen Fingerzeig geben könnten, zum Beispiel:

sometimes none. The fact that the figure for deaths began to rise at the end of November 1632, as the following graph shows, must have attracted attention and caused alarm: Even a medically untrained eye can see immediately that an infectious disease broke out here, reaching its climax in March 1633 and ending in July. Since this documentary list of deaths cannot be reconciled with the figures in the CHRONICLE, attempts have been made to discredit it, as if the overburdened priests had been careless in registering deaths; yet they registered none at all. Furthermore register entries by the priests (e.g. baptisms performed without music) always use the correct saints' names from the Roman missal, while all others use the informal names, e.g. Apelania (Apollonia), Duredea (Dorothea), Mathoyss (Matthias) etc. Yet we do not know whether all the registered names were also victims of the plague; in any case, the register of baptisms does not show any children who died prematurely. Very rarely there are additional remarks which give us a hint, e.g.

12. 12. 1632 Agata Lindauerin, serving maid of Kolgrueb.
21. 12. Hansen Stickhl, verger.
28. 1. 1633 H. Primus Christeiner, priest of this place.
19. 3. H. Marcelus Fattiga, former priest.

While the last three were, so to speak, victims of their profession, the additional particulars for the serving maid Agatha Lindauer show the village where the plague also raged. PAUHOFER himself made his last entry on 26th February 1633, then the plague took the pen from his hand because on 18th April he himself appears among the dead. On the same page, i. e. not an insertion, another person, namely the school master, GEORG LUDWIG, completed the series after the plague ended, in a pedantically neat list with the names elegantly one under the other. The fact that he placed the last death on 27th February at the beginning shows that he intended the list to be complete. In the marriage register PAUHOFER had listed nine couples for 1631, while in 1632 there were five couples in the first half-year. For 1633 LUDWIG can offer fifteen couples of whom eleven however went to the altar only after Whitsun. There is no marriage boom as in Kohlgrub because the plague ended earlier and could not claim so many victims as in Kohlgrub. This should please everyone who honestly believes in the power of a vow; 1633 is undoubtedly the year of the vow but we cannot commit ourselves to a specific date. The date given by the CHRONICLE (Feast of the

Während die drei Letztgenannten sozusagen Berufsopfer waren, deutet der Zusatz bei dem Dienstmädchen Agatha Lindauer auf das Dorf hin, in dem die Pest auch wütete. PAUHOFER selber machte am 26. 2. 1633 seine letzte Eintragung; dann nahm ihm die Pest sozusagen die Feder aus der Hand; am 18. 4. erscheint er selbst unter den Toten. Auf dem gleichen Blatt, also nicht auf einem *Einschiebsel,* hat ein anderer, nämlich der Schulmeister GEORG LUDWIG, nach dem Ende der Pest in einer pedantisch saubereren Liste schön untereinander die Reihe ergänzt. Daß er auf Vollständigkeit bedacht war, ersieht man daraus, daß er den letzten Todesfall im Februar (27. 2.) voransetzte. Auf der Hochzeitsliste hatte PAUHOFER für 1631 9 Paare aufgeführt; 1632 waren es 5 Paare im 1. Halbjahr. LUDWIG kann für 1633 mit 15 Paaren aufwarten, von denen 11 allerdings erst nach Pfingsten an den Altar treten. Es gibt keinen Hochzeitsboom wie in Kohlgrub, denn die Pest wurde früher gestoppt und konnte nicht soviel Opfer fordern wie in Kohlgrub. Das

sollte doch jeden freuen, der ehrlich an die Kraft eines Gelübdes glaubt; 1633 ist zweifelsohne das Gelübdejahr; auf ein Datum können wir uns nicht festlegen. Der von der CHRONIK angegebene Termin (Fest der Apostel Simon und Judas Thaddäus 28. 10. 1633) ist unverständlich, zumal die Verehrung des Apostels Judas Thaddäus als Nothelfer in Bayern und Österreich erst im 18. Jahrhundert nachweisbar ist. Ein Gelübde kann jeder einzelne für sich ablegen und erfüllen; wenn es aber eine Gemeinschaft tut, muß es auch von der Gemeinschaft erfüllt werden können. Oberammergau gelobte nicht etwas, was die Wohlhabenden betraf (z. B. Bau einer Kapelle), sondern woran alle, arm und reich, persönlich teilhaben sollten: ein heiliges Spiel, ja, das heiligste Spiel, das sie kannten und gelegentlich auch gesehen haben konnten, z. B. 1600 und 1615 in der Stadt Weilheim, ein Passionsspiel. Und bei ihnen verkündeten die Lebenden über den Gräbern der Toten den Sieg des Lebens über den Tod.

Bühne auf der Passionswiese (1830)

Apostles Simon and Thaddeus, 28th October 1633) is incomprehensible, particularly as veneration of the Apostle Thaddeus as an auxiliary saint in Bavaria and Austria can only be proved in the 18th century.
Any individual can make a vow and fulfil it on his own behalf, but when a community does so it must be fulfilled by the whole community. Oberammergau did not vow to do something which concerned the well-to-do (e.g. building a chapel), but something in which everyone, poor and rich, could participate personally: a holy play, indeed the holiest play which they knew and may even have seen occasionally, e.g. in 1600 and 1615 in the town of Weilheim, a Passion Play. And in their case the living, over the graves of the dead are proclaimed the complete victory of life over death.

Kreuzigungsszene (1850)

DAS ERSTE PASSIONSSPIEL | THE FIRST PASSION PLAY

Passionsspiele waren im Mittelalter aus lateinischen Osterspielen zu wahren Großraumspielen geworden, wo unter Einbeziehung von Gebäuden, Straßen und vor allem Plätzen dem leseunkundigen Volk von Land und Stadt der Verlauf der Erlösung in der Muttersprache vorgeführt wurde. In der Reformation – Bilderstürmer waren oft auch Spielstürmer – hatten diese Spiele viel an Boden verloren, dies aber durch eine Art von Rückzug in kleinere Städte und Märkte wettgemacht, wo sie vielerorts als Teil der Karwochenfeier mit dem Kreuzweg in der Form einer Prozession weiterlebten, nicht immer zur Freude der geistlichen und weltlichen Obrigkeit. Ein solches Spiel plante Oberammergau nicht, da es von vornherein den Spieltermin auf den Pfingstmontag und damit weit weg von der Karwoche festlegte, nicht zuletzt auch aus klimatischen Gründen. Selbst wenn wir die besondere Spielbegabung und -freude der Gebirgsbewohner ins Gewicht fallen lassen, so muß es doch einen tieferen Grund gerade für dieses Spielgelübde geben. Die Abschrift des ältesten Spieltextes von 1662 gibt uns einen Hinweis. Es wird mehrmals ein Prologus auf die Bühne geschickt, um das Spiel an geeigneten Stellen zum Zweck belehrender Betrachtung zu unterbrechen. Beim Tod Christi, nachdem die Erde gebebt hat und die Priester wegen des in zwei Teile zerrissenen Vorhangs in den Tempel geeilt sind, beginnt der Prologus, ohne jede weitere Einleitung Christus mit der Ehernen Schlange zu vergleichen, die Moses auf Gottes Geheiß aufgerichtet hat, damit die von feurigen Schlangen tödlich gebissenen Juden in der Wüste durch den Aufblick zu ihr wieder gesundeten. So habe uns Jesus von den Bissen der höllischen Schlange, d. h. von den Sünden geheilt; die tödlichen Wunden der Pest liegen nahe, zumal dies das einzige »Vorbild« im ersten Text ist. Noch 1787 wurde diese Wüstenszene in der neuen Oberammergauer Pfarrkirche unter der Orgelempore als Deckengemälde in Erinnerung gebracht.

Im Gegensatz zu allen anderen Passionsspielen war weder die katholische Pfarrei noch eine religiöse Vereinigung, sondern die Dorfgemeinschaft Träger und Erbe des Passionsgelübdes. Zwar hatte der Propst von Rottenbuch im Ammergau die Seelsorger zu stellen, aber der Abt von Ettal war zuständig für alles Weltliche, wie z. B. die Gemeindefinanzen. Erst nachdem die

In the Middle Ages Passion plays developed from Latin Easter plays into true open-air plays in which the process of salvation was presented to the illiterate people of town und country in their mother tongue, making use of buildings, streets and, above all, squares. In the Reformation (iconoclasts were often also against the plays) these plays lost a great deal of ground, but made this up by, so to speak, retreating into small towns and markets where in many places they continued as part of the Holy Week celebrations with the way of the Cross in the form of a procession, not always to the delight of the spiritual and secular authorities. Oberammergau did not plan a play of this kind, because from the beginning the date of the play was fixed for Whit Monday, which was much later than Holy Week, and not least for reasons of climate. Even allowing for the mountain dwellers' special talent for acting and pleasure in it, there must be a deeper reason for this particular vow to perform a play. The copy of the oldest text of the play dated 1662 gives us a hint. Several times a Prologue is sent onto the stage to interrupt the play at suitable points for the purpose of instructive meditation. At Christ's death, after the earth shakes and the priests hurry into the temple because the curtain was torn in two, the Prologue begins, without further introduction, to compare Christ with the brazen serpent which Moses raised at God's command so that the Jews who had been fatally bitten by fiery serpents in the desert would be healed by looking up at it. In the same way, said the Prologue, Jesus has healed us from the bite of the infernal serpent, i.e. from sin: the fatal wounds of the plague are suggested, particularly as this is the only *"prefiguration"* in the first text. As late as 1787 this desert scene was recalled in the new parish church of Oberammergau as a ceiling painting under the organ gallery.

By contrast with all other Passion plays it was the village community, not the Catholic parish or a religious society, which was the upholder of and successor to the vow to perform the play. Although the Provost of Rottenbuch in Ammergau had to provide for the care of souls, the Abbot of Ettal was responsible for all secular matters, such as the parish finances. Only after the Six and the Twelve had obtained the permission of the Abbot of Ettal, because of the

Sechs und die Zwölf wegen der sich auf Jahrzehnte erstreckenden außerordentlichen Kosten des Spieles die Zustimmung des Abtes von Ettal eingeholt hatten, konnten sie ohne Verzögerung ihr Gelöbnis machen; die Wirkung trat offensichtlich rasch ein. Am 19. 3. 1633 war der Pfarrer Marcellus Fatiga (aus der Sicht des später schreibenden LUDWIG »gewößener Pfarrer«) an der Pest gestorben, nachdem sein Vorgänger Primus Christeiner schon am 28. 1. an der gleichen Krankheit verschieden war. Aus diesen Tagen muß ein Schreiben stammen, das im Ettaler Klosterarchiv aufbewahrt wurde: »Anno 1633 bey der Kranckheit des Herrn Pfarrers auf begehren des H. Propstes ein Priester von uns auf einige Tage hinabgeschickt worden.« Im Registraturschrank des Ettaler Richters befand sich ein nicht abgelehntes Gesuch: »Die Ammergauer bitten, daß man ihnen einige Nothwendigkeiten zur Spielung des Passion geben wolle.« In dem zugehörigen Renner (Nachschlagehilfe) heißt es positiv: »Passionsspielung halber erlangen die Ammergauer verschiedene Nothwendigkeiten.« Leider ist das Gesuch nicht datiert und vom Staat im 19. Jahrhundert vermutlich mit vielen anderen Akten vernichtet worden. Das Verzeichnis des Ettaler Klosterarchives von 1700 kennt aber einige gleichzeitige ähnliche Gesuche:

»21. 11. 1616: Ein anderer von der Gemain daselbst bittet um Holz aus dem Graswang zu der Gemain wegen underer Prugg.« (Die Unterhaltungspflicht der durchs Dorf führenden Rottstraße lag auf den anrainenden Häusern; die Brücke über die Ammer mußte aus großen Stämmen gefertigt werden, wie sie der Gemeindewald nicht aufwies.) »27. 7. 1629: Ein Ammergauer bittet supplicative um holz aus dem Graswang um stammgelt.« (Ein Höldrich wollte sein Haus vergrößern.) Man war also bei besonderen Bauvorhaben auf die starken Stämme aus dem Klosterwald im Graswangtal angewiesen. Kostüme für ein kleines Theaterstück konnte man sich damals aus Rottenbuch und Schongau ausleihen, aber für ein Spiel im Freien, wo größere Mengen wie Jesus mit den Zwölfen, der Hohe Rat, Pilatus mit Gefolge, das Volk vor Pilatus auftraten, brauchte man eine wetterfeste und geräumige Bühne. Jenes undatierte Gesuch hatte nur für das Jahr 1634 einen Sinn, denn 1637 folgte auf den altersschwachen und resignierenden Abt GOPPELZRIEDER der erst 27 Jahre alte energische Abt IGNAZ RUEF, ein ausgezeichneter Rechner und Hausvater. Mit ihm befand sich Oberammergau bereits ab 1638 wegen vieler Fragen in einem Prozeß, der erst 1684 unter dem 4. Nachfolger des Abtes GOPPELZ-

exceptional expenses of the play spreading over decades, were they able to make their vow without hesitation. It seems to have taken effect quickly. On 19th March 1633 the parish priest Marcellus Fatiga (described as *"former priest"* by LUDWIG who was writing later) died of the plague after his predecessor, Primus Christeiner, had suffered the same fate on 28th January. A letter preserved in the monastery archives of Ettal must date from this period: *"In the year 1633 during the priest's illness, at the request of the Provost a priest was sent down by us for several days."* In the filing cabinet of the Ettal judge there was a request which was not refused: *"The people of Ammergau ask that they be given some necessities for playing the Passion."* In the accompanying index it is stated positively: *"For the Passion Play the people of Oberammergau should be given various necessities."* Unfortunately the request was undated and was presumably destroyed by the State in the 19th century together with many other documents. However, the index of the Ettal Monastery archives of 1700 contains several similar requests of the same period: *"21st November 1616: Another person from the same community asks for wood from the Graswang for the community for the lower bridge."* (The obligation of maintaining the highway leading

through the village rested with the adjoining houses; the bridge over the Ammer must have been made of large trunks of a kind which did not grow in the parish forest.) *"27th July 1629: A man from Ammergau petitions for wood from the Graswang in return for timber money."* (A member of the Höldrich family wanted to enlarge his house.) Consequently for special building projects people had to rely on the strong trunks from the monastery forest in the Graswang valley. At that time costumes for a small play could be borrowed from Rottenbuch and Schongau but for a play in the open air, where large crowds appeared such as Jesus with the Twelve Apostles, the High Council, Pilate and his retinue, and the people before Pilate, a spacious weatherproof stage was needed. The abovementioned undated request could have related only to the year 1634 because in 1637 the senile Abbot GOPPELZRIEDER, who was compelled to retire, was succeeded by the energetic Abbot IGNAZ RUEF, who was only 27 and an excellent book-keeper and father of the house. As soon as 1638 Oberammergau was involved in legal proceedings with him concerning many questions and the dispute only came to an end in 1684 with a settlement under the fourth successor of Abbot GOPPELZRIEDER. In

RIEDER mit einem Vergleich enden sollte. Danach blieb der Wald im Graswangtal nach wie vor im Eigentum des Klosters, wogegen dieses zugestand, daß jährlich etwa 12 Angehörige der 4 Hofmäder gleichheitlich gegen Bezahlung auf Zuweisung von Stämmen durch die Ettaler Holzknechte rechnen konnten. Während des ganzen Prozesses (1638–1684) war obiges Gesuch sicher unangebracht, nachher nicht mehr nötig. Daß sich Oberammergau 1634 eine große Bühne besorgen mußte, spricht außerdem auch gegen die in keiner Weise belegte Vermutung, es hätte schon früher Passion gespielt und jetzt nur den Zehnjahresturnus gelobt.

Es ist auch unwahrscheinlich, daß eine ganze Passion in der Oberammergauer Kirche aus der gotischen Zeit, die noch DAISENBERGER als viel zu klein bezeichnet, aufgeführt wurde; höchstens wurde ein einfaches Osterspiel gewagt. Daß nunmehr auf dem Friedhof gespielt wurde, darf nicht als pietätlos bezeichnet werden, denn alpenländische Friedhöfe besaßen damals noch keine Steindenkmäler, sondern nur einfache schmiedeeiserne oder, wie im Falle eines Schnitzerdorfes naheliegend, hölzerne Kreuze, die sich alle zehn Jahre einmal entfernen und wieder anbringen ließen. Die erste Bühne mußte nach Art einer mittelalterlichen Simul-

tanbühne breit und tief sein, um mehrere Schauplätze gleichzeitig oder wenigstens rasch hintereinander benützen zu können. Im Text von 1662 heißt es öfters z. B. beim Hohen Rat oder beim Ölberg »welches zuvor soll zugerichtet werden«; Das Gemach des Herodes hat einen »töbich« als Hintergrund. 1634 gab es ohnehin nur einheimisches Publikum, denn die Oberammergauer hätten vermessen, ja selbstmörderisch gehandelt, wenn sie ihre Sperren gelockert hätten. Noch nach dem ersten Spiel starb in Ettal der aus München stammende Diakon WILHELM HÖRTNIT an der Pest. 1664 begrüßte der Prologus zwar einige geistliche und weltliche Würdenträger (Herren), aber auch Burger und Bauern, die »zugegen stan«, und bittet alle um Nachsicht bei etwaigen Fehlern, denn sie seien nur »grobe paurs leith«. So sehr waren sie sich damals noch des Abstandes von den gewohnten städtischen Aufführungen bewußt. Der Nachtrag zur Aufführung von 1674 (»ist gar glickhlich abgangen«) zeigt, daß die Passion immer noch ein Wagnis für das Dorf war.

Das Hilfegesuch an Ettal bezog sich sicher nicht nur auf das Holz für die Bühne, sondern auch auf den *Text*. Der 1600 und 1615 in Weilheim benützte Text des dortigen Stadtpfarrers ÄLBL, der anderweitig viel abgeschrieben und gespielt

accordance with this, the forest in the Graswang valley remained the monastery's property, in return for which the monastery made the concession that each year about twelve members of the four *"Hofmäder"* on an equal basis could expect to be allocated trunks by the Ettal woodcutters against payment. During the entire proceedings (1638–1684) the above-mentioned application was certainly inappropriate, and afterwards it was unnecessary. The fact that Oberammergau had to procure a large stage in 1634 also rebuts the presumption, which is in no way supported, that it had performed Passion plays earlier and now vowed only the ten-yearly rotation. It is also improbable that an entire Passion play was performed in the Gothic church of Oberammergau, which even DAISENBERGER described as much too small. At the most a simple Easter play was ventured. The fact that plays were henceforth given in the churchyard should not be considered irreverent because at that time churchyards in Alpine regions did not have stone crosses but simple wrought-iron crosses or, obviously in the case of a village of woodcarvers, wooden crosses which could be removed and put back once every ten years. The first stage must have been wide and deep in the manner of a

medieval simultaneous stage to enable several settings to be used simultaneously or at least in quick succession. The 1662 text often contains the stage direction, e.g. in the scenes with the High Council or on the Mount of Olives, *"which must be prepared beforehand"*; and Herod's apartment has a *"tapestry"* as background. In any case in 1634 the spectators were only local people because it would have been foolhardy, indeed suicidal, for the villagers of Oberammergau to lift their road blocks. Even after the first play the deacon WILHELM HÖRTNIT, who originated from Munich, died of the plague in Ettal. In 1664 the Prologue greeted several ecclesiastical and secular dignitaries (gentlemen) as well as townspeople and country people who were standing to watch, and begged everyone for their indulgence for any mistakes, because they were only *"rough country folk"*, so conscious were they even then of the difference from the customary performances in towns. The postscript to the 1674 performance *("it went off successfully")* shows that the Passion Play was still a venturous undertaking for the village.

The request to Ettal for help no doubt related not only to timber for the stage, but also to the text. Because of the village's isolation at the time, the text which had been

wurde, war anscheinend in der damaligen Isolation nicht greifbar. Was tatsächlich 1634 gespielt wurde, wissen wir nicht, aber die Hartnäckigkeit, mit der die Oberammergauer auch später am Wortlaut ihres Textes festhielten, läßt vermuten, daß eine vom Schulmeister GEORG KAISER gefertigte Abschrift »1662 der alt Passion« trotz der Nachschrift »Ist widerumben renoviert und beschrieben worden im Jar nach der gnadenreichen Geburtt Christi 1662« im großen und ganzen den ältesten Text enthält. Daß dieses Buch tatsächlich als Regiebuch in Gebrauch war, ergibt sich nicht nur aus manchen Schmutzspuren, sondern besonders aus ehemals rötlichen Flecken auf den Seiten 107 und 108, wo eine Anweisung besagt: »Der speer soll sein wie ein sprizen, darin soll rote farbe sein, wenn er sticht, daß man sech alß wan das bluet heraus rint.« Das scheint bei offenem Buch nur allzu erfolgreich ausprobiert worden zu sein. Es war anscheinend auch das Handexemplar des zweimal mit Tinte eingetragenen Spielleiters JOHANN JAKOB WIRMSEER, der übrigens 1710 das Deckenfresko der Unterammergauer Pfarrkirche signierte.

1880 gelang AUGUST HARTMANN, dem Direktor der Münchener Hof- und Staatsbibliothek, der Nachweis, daß dieses Passionsspiel kein Originalwerk war, sondern eine Kompilation (Zusammensetzung) aus wenigstens zwei älteren Spielen, die er überdies in seiner Bibliothek verwahrte. Das Rückgrat des Spieles bildete ein etwa 1450 geschriebenes schwäbisches Volksschauspiel des Benediktinerklosters St. Ulrich und Afra in Augsburg (das aber nach neuesten Forschungen nur ein unvollständiger Auszug aus einem älteren und größeren schwäbisch-tirolischen Passionsspiel ist). Es wurde etwas gewaltsam bajuwarisiert und mehr und mehr mit Versen aufgefüllt, die aus einem 1566 in Augsburg gedruckten Passionsspiel des dortigen Meistersingers und Schneidermeisters SEBASTIAN WILD stammten. WILDs Spiel allein hätte nicht genügt, denn als Protestant ließ er die Figur der Gottesmutter ganz weg, desgleichen das unter den Reformierten selbst strittige Abendmahl; sogar den Kreuzweg und die Kreuzigung mußte er aus technischen Gründen – ihm stand nur ein Meistersingerpodium in der Augsburger Jakobuskirche zur Verfügung – weglassen bzw. durch einen langatmigen Botenbericht des Centurio vor Pilatus und durch derbe Späße der vier Grabwächter ersetzen. Der Kompilator nahm beides und erzielte damit eine ungeschickte Motivverdoppelung (z. B. Mariens Klage und die diese ersetzen sollenden Klagen der begleitenden Frauen); er

used in Weilheim in 1600 and 1615, written by the town priest ÄLBL and frequently copied and performed in other places, was evidently not available. We do not know what was actually performed in 1634, but the stubbornness with which the villagers of Oberammergau later adhered to the wording of their text indicates that a copy of the *"Old Passion"* made in 1662 by the schoolmaster GEORG KAISER contains by and large the oldest text, in spite of the postscript: *"Revised and rewritten anno Domini 1662."* The fact that this book was actually used as a prompt book is shown not only by the many traces of dirt but also from some once reddish spots on pages 107 and 108 where there is the following direction: *"the spear should be like a sprinkler with red dye, when it strikes it looks as if the blood runs from it."* This seems to have been tried out all too successfully when the book was open. Evidently it was also the personal copy of the director JOHANN JAKOB WIRMSEER, whose name is entered twice in ink, and who incidentally signed the ceiling fresco in the parish church of Unterammergau in 1710.

In 1880 AUGUST HARTMANN, the director of the Munich Court and State Library, found proof that this Passion Play was not an original work but a compilation of at least two older plays which were also in the Library. The backbone of the play was formed by a Swabian folk play, written about 1450, from the Benedictine monastery of St. Ulrich and Afra in Augsburg (which however according to the latest research is only an incomplete extract from an older and longer Swabian-Tyrolean Passion play). It was rather drastically rewritten in the Bavarian dialect and gradually filled out with verses originating from a Passion play printed in Augsburg in 1566, written by SEBASTIAN WILD, a mastersinger and master tailor of that town. WILD's play alone would have been inadequate because as a Protestant he left out the figure of the Mother of God entirely, likewise the Last Supper, which is disputed among members of the Reformed Church themselves. He even had to omit the way of the Cross and the Crucifixion for technical reasons—all that was available was a mastersinger's podium in the Church of St. James in Augsburg—and replace them by a long-winded report by the Centurion to Pilate and by coarse jokes of the guards at the Tomb. The compiler took both episodes, thereby achieving a clumsy duplication of subject matter (e.g. Mary's lament and the laments of the accompanying women, which are intended to replace it); he added several other

fügte noch manches hinzu, dessen Herkunft unbekannt bleibt, so das etwa 200 Verse umfassende »Ungerechte Gericht«, in dem der Hohe Rat mit Kayphas und Pilatus zusammen das Todesurteil fällt, und zwar mit 15 gegen 5 Stimmen. 1581 war über Flugblätter die sensationelle Nachricht durchs Abendland gegangen, man habe im Sarkophag einer Ruine in Aquila (Mittelitalien) das hebräische Protokoll dieser Sitzung gefunden. Vergebens erklärte Rom dieses Protokoll 1588 als Fälschung; es war bereits in die Spiele eingegangen. – Die Reden der Vorväter aus der Hölle bilden einen sehr alten Block für sich und dürften aus Oberammergau selbst stammen. Hier wird auf die im Volksschauspiel sonst sehr beliebte Technik verzichtet, dem nachfolgenden Sprecher durch den ersten Teil eines Paarreimes das Stichwort bzw. den Stichvers für den zweiten Teil zu geben.

Sprachlich war dieser Urtext noch 1662 sehr rückständig, d. h. mittelalterlich und hart deklamierbar, aber das Endergebnis war doch ein komplettes Passionsspiel, wie es 1633 gelobt wurde. Hätte der Verfasser des Textes Zeit bis 1644 gehabt, wäre es sicher möglich gewesen, mit etwas weitaus Besserem anzutreten. Auch vom sprachlichen Gesichtspunkt aus bleibt es bei 1634. Die mündliche Überlieferung, wie sie sich in der CHRONIK erhalten hat, kennt ebenfalls kein anderes Jahr, mag sie auch noch so viel Legendenwerk darum ranken.

things the origin of which is unknown, for instance the *"Unjust Judgment"* containing about 200 lines, in which the High Council with Caiaphas and Pilate together pronounce the death sentence by 15 votes to 5. In 1581 handbills appeared in the West announcing the sensational news that the Hebrew record of this meeting had been found in a sarcophagus in some ruins in Aquila (Central Italy). In vain did Rome declare the record a forgery in 1588: it had already been taken into the Play. The speeches of the forefathers from Hell form a very old section of their own and no doubt originate from Oberammergau itself. No use was made here of the technique, which was otherwise very popular in folk plays, of giving the next speaker, by means of the first part of a rhyming couplet, the cue for the second part. Linguistically this original text was even in 1662 very outdated, i.e. medieval and hard to declaim, but the final result was nevertheless a complete Passion Play as had been vowed in 1633. If the writer of the text had had time until 1644 it would certainly have been possible to start with something much better. From the language viewpoint 1634 remains the first year of the Play. The oral tradition, as preserved in the CHRONICLE, refers to no other year either, however many myths it may invent on the subject.

Darsteller (1850)

WACHSTUM

1674 werden dem Textbuch einige Seiten neuen Textes durch GEORG KAISER eingefügt. Das Weilheimer Spiel des Pfarrers ÄLBL ist anscheinend zugänglich geworden; aus ihm werden einige Verse entlehnt, so die lustige Anfangsszene mit dem kleinen Teufel, der nach dem Prolog auf die Bühne springt und allen, die das mißliebige fromme Spiel stören, die besondere Gunst seines höllischen Herrn verspricht; die ältesten Teufel stammen übrigens aus WILDs Spiel.

Volkskundlich wichtiger ist die so genannte »Urlaubsnehmung«, d. h. der Abschied Christi von seiner tiefbetrübten Mutter Andererseits wird auch die Szene eingefügt, da der Auferstandene ihr privat erscheint, angekündigt vom Engel Gabriel durch den überall in der Kirche die ganze Osterzeit hindurch gesungenen Gruß: »Regina caeli, laetare« (Freu dich, du Himmelskönigin). Noch wichtiger: das betrachtende Element wächst. Fünfmal trifft ein Dialog zwischen der menschlichen Seele und einem Engel. Gerne würde man diese Szenen AUGUSTIN GRIENINGER aus Rottenbuch, der gerade 1674 Pfarrer von Oberammergau war, zuschreiben, wenn nur sein Erbauungsschriftchen »Christi Schmach = Schuel. Das ist Erinnerungen der unserm Hailandt auf Erden zuegefügten und in höchster Geduld erlittenen Schmachen, cum appendice (Anhang) ein Liebsgespräch mit Christo anzustellen. Augsburg 1682« aufzufinden wäre. Aber es ist verschollen. – Auch Musik wird eingeschaltet, wenn auch nicht gesagt wird, was da jeweils gesungen wird; immerhin wird das Auftreten von Respektspersonen (Hoher Rat und Pilatus) durch Trompeten markiert. Das Spiel ist angewachsen, der Dienst am Zuschauer beginnt: »Solln hin firo fir die zusechende Persohnen alzeit Süz gemacht werden.« Als nächste archivalische Notiz haben wir den Eintrag des P. ENGELBERT SARTORI aus München (1664–1722) in seinem Tagebuch; »13. 5. 1704: habendie Ober-Ammergauer Passionem Domini exhibiert.« Daß diese Aufführung am Pfingstmontag 1704 mitten im Spanischen Erbfolgekrieg glückte, darf nicht erstaunen, da gerade um diese Zeit das Ettaler Territorium einigermaßen friedlich lebte. Da aber ein solches Spiel längere Vorbereitungen erforderte, kann man sich nicht so sehr auf diese Kampfpause berufen, sondern muß den eisernen Willen des Dorfes bewundern, das nun einmal gelobte Spiel unter allen Umständen

DEVELOPMENT

In 1674 several pages of new text were added to the Play by GEORG KAISER. Evidently the Weilheim play by ÄLBL had become accessible because several verses are borrowed from it, for instance, the funny opening scene with the small devil who springs on to the stage after the prologue and promises the special favour of his infernal master to all those who spoil the unacceptably devout play. Incidentally, the oldest devils originate from WILD's play.

More important from the viewpoint of folklore is the so-called "leavetaking", i.e. Christ's farewell to his sorrowing mother. Another addition is the scene where the risen Christ appears to her in private, announced by the Angel Gabriel by the greeting which is sung everywhere in the church throughout Easter: "Regina caeli, laetare" (Rejoice, Queen of Heaven). Even more important is the increased contemplative element. On five occasions there is a dialogue between the human soul and an angel. We would willingly attribute these scenes to AUGUSTIN GRIENINGER of Rottenbuch, who was the parish priest of Oberammergau in 1674, if it were possible to find his small devotional book "Christi Schmach-Schuel. Recollections of the mortification caused to our Saviour on Earth and suffered with the greatest endurance, with an appendix to begin a loving discourse with Christ. Augsburg 1682." But it has disappeared. Music was also added, but it is not said what was sung; at any rate, the appearance of persons commanding respect (High Council, Pilate) was marked by trumpets. The Play began to grow and facilities were provided for the spectators: "In future seats should be made for all the persons watching." As the next documentary reference we have is the entry by Father ENGELBERT SARTORI of Munich (1664–1722) in his diary: "13th May 1704: The villagers of Ober-Ammergau performed the Passion of the Lord." It is no surprise that this successful performance took place on Whit Monday 1704 in the middle of the War of the Spanish Succession, because the territory of Ettal led a more or less peaceful existence precisely at this more or less peaceable time. However, as such a Play required lengthy preparation, too much emphasis should not be placed on this lull in the fighting and we must admire the iron will of the village to perform the Play, once the vow had been made, on the due date, come

termingerecht zu halten. Freilich geraten wir erneut mit der CHRONIK in Konflikt, die da schreibt: *»Alsdan ist diese Tragödie von 1634 gehalten worden, bis auf 1680. Damals hat man sie auf die zehn Jahre verlegt und ist darnach allzeit so gehalten worden.«* 1680 ist bei dieser Rückerinnerung von 1733 entschieden zu früh; der Grund dürfte ein ganz anderer sein. Anno 1300 hatte Papst Bonifaz VIII. jedes volle Jahrhundert der christlichen Zeitrechnung zu einem Jubiläumsjahr erklärt, bei dem an den vier römischen Hauptbasiliken sonst vermauerte Gnadenpforten geöffnet wurden; der ganze christliche Erdkreis feierte diese Jubeljahre auf seine Weise mit. Unter ausdrücklicher Berufung darauf hatte Weilheim anno 1600 Passion gespielt und sie eben jetzt im Jahre 1700 an den Kartagen wiederholt. Wenn Oberammergau am Pfingstmontag im Jahre 1700 nachkam, war dies keine Konkurrenz.

Als nächstes liegt uns ein undatiertes Spielerverzeichnis – es kann auch ein Besetzungsplan sein – vor, das sich durch Vergleich mit den damaligen Oberammergauer Familienbüchern eindeutig auf das Jahr 1710 festlegen läßt. Also dürfte im Jahre 1710 das erste normale Zehnerjahr sein.

In der nachfolgenden Zeit wurde der Text mehrfach abgeschrieben, aber davon sind uns nur einzelne Bündel (Faszikel) erhalten, die jeweils ein Drittel des Textes umfassen und im Privatarchiv des Hauses RICHARD LANG in Oberammergau wohlverwahrt sind. Durch Schriftvergleich ergab sich, daß das älteste Bündel, nämlich ein dritter Teil, von dem Sekretär MICHAEL LIEPART (1690–1738) des Abtes PLACIDUS SEIZ geschrieben wurde; seine bizarre Handschrift ist in vielen Briefprotokollen und Anfallbüchern bekundet. Für welchen Ettaler schrieb dieser Ettaler? (Für Oberammergauer hatte stets der dortige Schulmeister oder Spielleiter geschrieben.) Seit 1711 baute Ettal eine sogenannte »Ritterakademie«, d. h. eine Schule für Adelige auf, die sich bald eines guten Rufes und großen Zulaufes erfreute; die gymnasialen Fächer konnten die Patres selber geben, aber für die »cavaliersmäßigen« mußten sie teure weltliche Lehrer anstellen. Seit 1713 stand der Schule und ihrem Theater ein ausgezeichneter Mann vor, der aus Weilheim gebürtige P. KARL BADER; auch BAADER geschrieben (1662–1731). Nach einer von Arthritis belasteten Jugend war er erst 1690 in Ettal eingetreten. 1697 war er nach Studium und Priesterweihe als erster Leiter des mit Ettals Hilfe begründeten fürstbischöflichen Lyzeums nach Freising gegangen, hatte dort 5 Jahre Poesie gelehrt, anschließend in Salzburg weitere

what may. Of course, there is conflict again with the CHRONICLE, which writes: *"After that the tragedy was given from 1634 every tenth year until 1680. Then it was moved to the final year of each decade and thereafter was always given in that way."* In specifying 1680 this recollection dated 1733 is much too early; the reason must have been quite different. In 1300 Pope Boniface VIII had declared every year completing a century of the Christian era to be a jubilee year, when the holy doors, which were otherwise walled up, in the four main Roman basilicas were opened. The whole Christian world celebrated these jubilee years in its own way. In 1600 Weilheim performed the Passion with express reference to this, and now repeated it in 1700 at Easter. When Oberammergau came later, on Whit Monday 1700, it was not in a spirit of complete competition.

Next we have an undated list of players—it may also be a cast list—which can undoubtedly be fixed at 1710 by comparing it with the Oberammergau family books of the time, which recorded births, marriages and deaths. Therefore 1710 must have been the first normal decennial.

Subsequently the text was copied out several times, but all that has come down to us are separate fascicles, each comprising one third of the text and now well preserved in the private archives of the old RICHARD LANG family in Oberammergau. A handwriting comparison has shown that the oldest fascicle, i.e. a one-third part, was written by MICHAEL LIEPART (1690–1738), secretary of the Abbot PLACIDUS SEIZ. His bizarre handwriting appears in many legal documents and deeds. He lived in Ettal, so for which other person in Ettal did he write? The village schoolmaster or producer had always written for Oberammergau. From 1711 Ettal was setting up an academy for the sons of noblemen which soon acquired a good reputation and attracted many students. The monks themselves could teach the classical subjects, but for the *"gentlemanly"* subjects they had to recruit expensive secular teachers. From 1713 the school and its theatre were headed by an excellent man, Father KARL BADER, also spelt BAADER, a native of Weilheim (1662–1731). After suffering serious arthritis in early life he entered Ettal in 1690. Then, after studying and taking holy orders, he went to Freising as the first director of the Prince Bishop's grammar school which had been founded with Ettal's help. There he taught poetry for five years and afterwards, in Salzburg, poetry for another three

3 Jahre Poesie und 8 Jahre Rhetorik, wobei er auch das Salzburger Akademietheater (lateinisch) führte, aber nicht minderes Lob für seine (nicht erhaltenen) Dichtungen in deutscher Sprache errang. Wichtiger als seine großen Schuldramen zum jeweiligen Schuljahrende sind die kleinen lateinischen Passionsspiele, die er in der Woche nach Ostern jeweils mit seinen Klassen anno 1705, 1707 und 1711 aufführte. 1720 stand er Oberammergau zur Verfügung; 1727 schied er durch Krankheit aus. Das uns erhaltene Bruchstück von 1720 verrät, daß er das Spiel in Akte und Auftritte eingeteilt hat, das Theater ein »großes Portal« mit einem beweglichen Vorhang besaß, also viele Szenen rasch hintereinander zu zeigen vermochte, abgesehen von dem festen Haus des Pilatus und der Hölle, die beide auch innere Spielflächen haben mußten. P. BADER sorgte dafür, daß die Szenen sich nicht »stießen«, d. h. zu rasch hintereinander oder gar gleichzeitig zu spielen waren. Nach Christi Tod auf Golgatha zieht sich z. B. alles so weit zurück, daß die Engel den guten Schächer in ein weißes Tuch wickeln und hinaustragen, die Teufel aber den bösen Schächer in einem Schubkarren in die Hölle kutschieren konnten; erst dann geht es weiter im Text. Die Emmausjünger dürfen nicht mehr bei der einen Seitenszene mit Jesus abgehen und gleich darauf bei der nächsten Szene zu den Aposteln hereinstürzen; Petrus hat einen längeren, kreuzgereimten Monolog dazwischen. Der gesamte Text wird gründlich überhobelt und geglättet, wobei das Verlegenheits- und Füllwörtchen »eben« allzu oft für Reimungen sorgen muß. Erstmals wird auch die »Urszene« der erlösten Väter in der Vorhölle angetastet; erstmals hören wir auch durch Randbemerkungen herbe Kritik aus dem Publikum, daß manches »geschwäz« zu lange dauere, besonders jenes der weinenden Frauen bei der Kreuzabnahme; hier rächt sich bereits die Motivverdopplung des Kompilators von 1662; »Man wird darob verdrissig, wie von mehrern die gemeine clag ist... doch aber, daß die haubtsach, wie es anjezo ist, gelassen werde.«

Wir kennen Ton und Schrift des Kritikers MAX ANTON ERLBÖCK. 1690 als Sohn eines Ettaler Richters in Oberammergau geboren, studierte er in Ettal und Salzburg Jus, hatte an mehreren Gerichten praktiziert, als der plötzliche Tod seiner Oberammergauer Braut seinem Leben eine Wendung zur Theologie gab. Statt seines Vaters Nachfolger wurde der junge Mann nun Frühmesser in Oberammergau. Er sah die Schäden des Passionsspieles, wollte die »hauptsach« retten, aber die Unzulänglichkeiten des Textes

years and rhetoric for eight years, also directing the Salzburg Academy Theatre (Latin) but achieving equal praise for his German poetry, which has not survived. More important than his long school dramas for the end of the respective school year are the small Latin Passion plays which he performed in the week after Easter with his classes of the years 1705, 1707 and 1711.

In 1720 he was available to Oberammergau, retiring in 1727 because of illness. The surviving fragment of 1720 shows that he divided the Play into acts and scenes, the stage possessed a *"large arched opening"* with a movable curtain, which meant that many scenes could be shown quickly one after the other, in addition to Pilate's fixed house and Hell itself, which must have both had internal acting areas. BADER ensured that the scenes did not *"collide"*, i.e. that they did not have to be played too quickly after each other or even simultaneously. After Christ's death at Golgotha, for instance, everyone withdraws so far that the angels can wrap the good bandit in a white cloth and carry him out, while devils take the bad bandit to Hell in a wheelbarrow; only then does the text continue. The disciples to whom the risen Christ appeared on the road to Emmaus are not allowed to exit with Him in one of the side scenes and then immediately rush in to the Apostles in the next scene. In between Peter has a long monologue with alternate rhymes. The entire text was thoroughly smoothed out and polished, the substitute word *"eben"* being all too often used to provide rhymes. For the first time the *"original scene"* of the redeemed forefathers in limbo was altered; for the first time also, from marginal notes, we read of sharp criticism from the public that a lot of *"talk"* lasts too long, particularly that of the weeping women at the descent from the Cross. This is the penalty paid for the duplication of subject matter by the 1662 compiler: *"People grow weary of it, and this is a general complaint by many ... but they say the main action should be left as it is and not made shorter."*

We know the style and handwriting of the critic MAX ANTON ERLBÖCK. Born in Oberammergau in 1690, the son of an Ettal judge, he studied law in Ettal and Salzburg and had practised at several courts when the sudden death of his bride from Oberammergau gave his life a turn towards theology. Instead of succeeding his father, the young man began to take the first morning mass in Oberammergau. He saw the damage done to the Passion Play and wanted to save the *"main*

beheben. Aus Ettal und dem Professorenkollegium der Ritterakademie konnte er keine Hilfe erwarten, denn die Gemeinde Oberammergau befand sich wiederum in einem Prozeß, der als »Bier- und Weinprozeß« (1727–1732) in die Ortsgeschichte Eingang fand. Die Gemeinde verlor diesen Prozeß und vergaß ihn wegen der damit verbundenen finanziellen Schwierigkeiten nicht so rasch.

Deshalb wandte sich ERLBÖCK an einen Rottenbucher Chorherrn, der fern in Oberauerbach bei Mindelheim Pfarrer war, sich aber als Dichter, Musiker und Prediger schon einen Namen gemacht hatte: P. ANSELM MANHARDT. Dieser war 1699 als Sohn des Klosterrichters im Augustinerstift Polling in Rottenbuch eingetreten, hatte sein poetisches Talent schon 1710 in Rottenbuch durch eine »Theatralische Vorstellung« für den Karfreitag bewiesen, die später als »Kreuzschuel« auch für Oberammergau noch Bedeutung erhalten sollte. Aber ihm ging es nicht so sehr um das Sprachliche, wie ERLBÖCK erhoffte, denn er wollte nur als »einfacher Gäu- und Bauernprediger den ungstudierten Leuten« das Evangelium predigen. Für das Sprachliche genügte ihm im allgemeinen die Weilheimer Passion; einen kräftigen Akzent der Handlung aber gewann er durch Übernahme des Höllenrates aus seiner »Kreuzschuel«: Gleich am Anfang beschließt die Hölle den Untergang Christi. Die Allegorien von Tod und Sünde stimmen bei, wobei letztere noch ihre Kinder Geiz und Neid ins Spiel bringt. Der Geiz hat allzeit einen prallen Geldbeutel und der Neid eine rote Schlange in der Hand zu halten. Das bedingt zugleich eine Spielerweiterung, denn in neuen Szenen mußten zuvor der Rat vom Neid und Judas vom Geiz erfaßt werden, bevor Judas seinen Meister um 30 Silberlinge verkaufen kann. Außerdem muß die Hölle sich in eigenen neuen Szenen informieren, beraten und (etwas zu früh) triumphieren. Die Spielhandlung wuchs also. Weniger Geschick bewies P. MANHARDT bei der Weiterentwicklung des betrachtenden Elementes. Freilich unterbrach er die Handlung nicht mehr an beliebiger Stelle, sondern nach den Akten, indem er aus dem nachfolgenden Akt ein paar typische Auftritte als sogenannte »Scenae mutae« (lebende Bilder, sozusagen Standphotos) vorausnahm und durch längere Strophen erklärte; das ging jeweils bis zu 6 Bildern, also mit den Zwischenstrophen bis zu 12 Strophen hintereinander. Das war beim lateinischen Drama vielleicht nützlich, hier aber als zwecklose Vorwegnahme der Spannung eher negativ. Einen glücklichen Griff tat er

action" while rectifying the shortcomings of the text. He could expect no help from Ettal and the teaching staff of the academy for the sons of noblemen because the parish of Oberammergau was again involved in a court action which has made its way into local history as the "Beer and Wine action" (1727–1732). The Parish lost the action and did not forget it quickly because of the resulting financial difficulties.

Therefore ERLBÖCK sought the help of a canon from Rottenbuch who was a priest in the distant village of Oberauerbach near Mindelheim, but had already made a name as a poet, musician and preacher, Father ANSELM MANHARDT. He had entered the monastery of Rottenbuch in 1699 as the son of the monastic judge in the Augustinian foundation of Polling, and gave proof of his poetic talent as early as 1710 in Rottenbuch by a "Theatrical Performance" for Good Friday which, as "Kreuzschuel" ("School of the Cross"), was later to become important for Oberammergau also. However he was not so concerned with the stylistic element, as ERLBÖCK hoped, because all he wanted to do was to preach the Gospel to "the unlearned people, as a simple local country preacher". For stylistic purposes generally he found the Weilheim Passion adequate, but he gained a powerful element in the action by including the Council of Hell from his "Kreuzschuel": right at the beginning Hell resolves upon the destruction of Christ. The allegories of Death and Sin approve, while the latter also brings her children Avarice and Envy into the Play. Avarice always has to hold a bulging moneybag and Envy a red serpent. At the same time this meant an expansion in the action, because in new scenes the Council must be overcome by Envy and Judas by Avarice before he can sell his Master for thirty pieces of silver. Furthermore in its own new scenes Hell has to obtain information, consult and (somewhat prematurely) triumph. Consequently the action grew. Father MANHARDT was less skilful in developing the meditative element. Naturally he did not interrupt the action at random but in the intervals between acts, by anticipating a few typical scenes from the following act as so-called "scenae mutae" (tableaux vivants or, so to speak, still photos) and explaining them in several long stanzas. This included up to six tableaux, i.e. with the intermediate stanzas, up to twelve stanzas one after another. This may have been useful in the Latin drama, but here it had a more negative effect as pointlessly anticipating the suspense. It

Jesus vertreibt die Händler aus den Tempelhallen (1890)

was a successful stroke of his to show the final tableau in two stages with the Lamb of the Apocalypse, Christ appearing again in Glory in the second tableau.

It is surprising that he went to Oberammergau as parish priest only at Easter 1730 and actually could make no further alterations. Certainly he had many discussions, but too late because in 1732 he was moved to Hohen Peissenberg where he preached and wrote extensively as a pilgrims' priest. He did not keep up a connection with Oberammergau so that in 1740 ERLBÖCK had to seek the assistance of the then priest, CLEMENS PRASSER, with regard to the verse improvements which were still necessary. However, shortly after the Passion Play, PRASSER was elected provost of Rottenbuch and had other cares from then on.

Christus vor Pilatus (1880)

mit dem in zwei Phasen gezeigten Schlußbild mit dem apokalyptischen Lamm, wobei beim zweiten Bild Christus nochmals in der Glorie aufzutreten hatte.

Es überrascht, daß er erst zu Ostern 1730 als Pfarrer nach Oberammergau kam und eigentlich nichts mehr ändern konnte. Sicher hat er viele Gespräche geführt, aber zu spät, denn 1732 wurde er auf den Hohen Peißenberg versetzt, wo er als Wallfahrtspriester eine fruchtbare Tätigkeit in Wort und Schrift entfaltete. Mit Oberammergau pflegte er keine Verbindung mehr, so daß sich ERLBÖCK 1740 wegen der noch immer nötigen Versverbesserungen an den damaligen Pfarrherrn CLEMENS PRASSER von Oberammergau wandte, der aber kurz nach dem Passionsspiel zum Propst von Rottenbuch gewählt wurde und fortan ganz andere Sorgen hatte.

PASSIO NOVA

Inzwischen hatte sich auch bei den Oberammergauern ein sozialer Aufstieg vollzogen; sie hätten sich nicht mehr als »grobe Paurs Leith« bezeichnet, denn sie waren recht weltläufig geworden, kamen als Handelsleute weit umher und wußten, was anderswo in der großen Welt bewundert oder belächelt wurde. Sie leisteten sich aus eigenen Kräften eine neue und große Dorfkirche, die nach langer Bauzeit 1749 eingeweiht werden konnte. Nun wollten sie auch eine entsprechende Erneuerung der Passion; eine starke Reformgruppe scheint sich gegen ERLBÖCK und die Verfechter des Alten durchgesetzt zu haben. In dem bereits damals über die lokalen Grenzen hinaus berühmten und als Fachmann des Schultheaters hervorgetretenen P. FERDINAND ROSNER aus Ettal fanden sie den rechten Mann, aus der alten Passion eine neue zu formen, wobei die Bezeichnung »neue« eher von den Gegnern dieser Passion gebraucht wurde. In Wirklichkeit hat der 1709 in Wien geborene und nunmehr etwa 40 Jahre alte P. ROSNER die Szenenfolge der bisherigen Passion fast ganz erhalten, gelegentlich – da seine Bühne Nebenbühnen überflüssig macht – Zwischenszenen auf der Vorbühne eingeschaltet, aber doch durch unerbittliche Strenge im Versmaß – etwas Einheitliches geschaffen, wobei auffällt, daß die oben erwähnte Technik der Weitergabe des Verses fast ganz aufhörte, die Oberammergauer also so selbständig geworden sind, daß sie eine solche Krücke nicht mehr brauchten. Nur bei ausgesprochen stimmungsmäßigen Passagen (z. B. Engel im Ölberghain) ließ er Kreuzreime zu. Das Höllenspektakel MANHARDTs mußte er wohl oder übel übernehmen, da es sehr bühnenwirksam war, jedoch verwandelte er die ausgesandten Allegorien von Neid und Geiz in gewöhnliche Menschen, z. B. den Neid in einen Abgesandten Galiläas (Vers 574: »So werden sie mich nicht erkennen«) und den Geiz in einen Genossen des Unterhändlers Amos (V. 928/9: »Damit man doch so leicht nicht merke, daß dich der geiz hierrinnen stärke«, rät er Judas, nur 30 Silberlinge zu verlangen). Dafür führt er neue Allegorien ein: die Verzweiflung, die Judas den Strick reicht (V. 3977), und am Schluß die Dankbarkeit mit ihrem Gefolge (»als Römisch gekleidet«), die eine Arie singt (V. 8435/8444). Der Prologus tritt nunmehr auf als »Schuzgeist diser Schaubühne, begleitet von 6 andren Schuzgeistern welche die

PASSIO NOVA

In the meantime the villagers of Oberammergau had risen socially. They would no longer have described themselves as "rough country folk" because they had become familiar with the ways of the world, they travelled far and wide as traders and knew what people in other parts of the world admired or found naive. From their own resources they built a large new village church which was consecrated in 1749 after a long period of construction. Now they also wished to restore the vitality of the Passion Play; a strong reform group seems to have succeeded against ERLBÖCK and the supporters of the old ways. In Father FERDINAND ROSNER of Ettal, who had emerged as a specialist in amateur theatre and whose fame had already spread beyond the local area, they found the right man for creating a new Passion from the old one, although the adjective "new" was used more by the opponents of this Passion. In reality ROSNER, who was born in Vienna in 1709 and was now about 40, retained the scene sequence of the existing Passion almost entirely, sometimes interpolating intermediate scenes on the proscenium stage because his stage makes side stages unnecessary. However, by means of an absolutely strict metre he created a homogeneous structure, and it is very noticeable that the above-mentioned technique of passing on the verse ceased almost completely, which means that the people of Oberammergau had become so independent that they no longer needed a device of that kind. He allowed alternate rhymes only in distinctly emotional passages (e.g. angel in the grove on the Mount of Olives). For better or worse he had to adopt MANHARDT's spectacle of Hell because it was very effective on the stage, but he changed the allegories Envy and Avarice into ordinary humans. Envy became an emissary of Galilee (verse 574: "Then they will not recognise me") and Avarice became a comrade of the go-between Amos (verses 928/9: "So that people should not notice so easily that Avarice fortified you in this", he advises Judas to ask for only 30 pieces of silver). On the other hand he introduced new allegories: Despair, who persuades Judas to despair and hands him the rope (verse 3977) and, at the end, Gratitude and her attendants ("dressed as Romans"), who sings an aria (verses 8435/8444). The Prologue now appears as "Tutelary Spirit of this stage, accompanied by six other tutelary

Werckhzeuge des Leyden Christi in denen Händen tragen«, der Ursprung des heutigen großen Chores. Der Schutzgeist spricht in Alexandrinern, einem Versmaß, das seinen Namen von einem französischen Alexanderepos hat und mit seinen 6 Jamben und einem leichten Einschnitt in der Mitte gerade für den Inhalt seiner etwas pathetischen Reden brauchbar war. Obwohl (oder gerade weil) ihn GOTTSCHED als Vers für das neue deutsche Drama empfohlen hatte, war er im Süden unbeliebt. Sonderbarerweise hat er sich durch ROSNERs meisterliche Handhabung auch in Bayern eingebürgert. Es ist trotzdem unsinnig, P. ROSNERs Passion als eine *»Alexandrinerpassion«* abzutun, denn von 8455 Versen sind nur 476 Alexandriner (5,6 %). Bis heute aber wirkt P. ROSNER dadurch nach, daß er die *»stummen Szenen«* seines Vorgängers abschaffte und statt ihrer sogenannte *»Vorbilder«* aus dem Alten Testament einführte, ebenfalls *»Stumme Bilder«,* völlig unbewegt und insofern in der bisherigen Linie liegend. Diese Rückbeziehung ist echt biblisch und geht auf Christus selbst zurück, der nicht nur die Eherne Schlange und den Jonas auf sich bezog, sondern ganz allgemein den Aposteln und den Emmausjüngern darlegte, was über seine Leiden *»von Mose und den Propheten ab«* vorhergesagt worden

Pater Ferdinand Rosner (1709–1778)

war. Für die kirchliche Tradition mag der Satz des hl. Augustinus stehen, wonach das Neue Testament im Alten verborgen liegt, letzteres aber im Neuen offenbar geworden ist *(novum in vetere latet, vetus in novo patet).* P. ROSNERs unmittelbare Quelle aber war das *spirits bearing the instruments of Christ's suffering",* the origin of the present-day large chorus. The Tutelary Spirit speaks in Alexandrines, a metre which takes its name from a French epic poem on Alexander and, with its six iambic feet and a slight pause in the middle, was particularly suitable for his rather impassioned speeches. Although (or precisely because) GOTTSCHED had recommended it as the metre for the new German drama, it was unpopular in the South of the country.

Strangely enough, it was adopted in Bavaria because of the masterly use made of it by ROSNER. Nevertheless it is absurd to dismiss Father ROSNER's Passion as an *"Alexandrine Passion",* because out of 8.455 verses only 476 are Alexandrines (5.6 %). However, ROSNER's influence is still felt today because he removed his predecessor's *"dumb scenes"* and replaced them by so-called *"prefiguration scenes"* from the old Testament, which were also *"tableaux vivants"* in the sense that they were completely motionless and therefore followed the previous model. This back reference is genuinely biblical and connects with Christ himself, who not only compared the brazen serpent and Jonas to himself but told the Apostles and disciples to whom he appeared on the road to Emmaus generally of what had been foretold of his sufferings *"by Moses and the prophets".* The church tradition is supported by St. Augustine's saying that the New Testament is concealed in the Old, while the latter is revealed in the New *("novum in vetere latet, vetus in novo patet").*

Schultheater, das mitunter im Prolog und den musikalischen Zwischenakten statt der Allegorien auch Einzelszenen oder zusammenhängende Nebenhandlungen aus dem Alten Testament brachte. Seine unbewegten Bilder kamen der barocken Schaulust ungemein entgegen; zunächst begnügte er sich mit 18 Bildern (je drei in einem »Chorus«, alle drei Strophen eines metrisch von den andern verschiedenen Liedes), aber schon 1760 scheint er sie vermehrt zu haben; in der vergebens gedruckten Perioche von 1770 hat er bereits 23 Vorbilder; Tölz war unersättlich und konsumierte an den Fastensonntagen und in der Karwoche nicht weniger als 37 Vorbilder; aus Tölz kam auch der Name für diese Art von Spiel: »Passion durch Betrachtungen«. Die Musik ist nicht erhalten, jedoch lassen sich sechs Vorbilder (zweimal je drei) auf zwei Melodien GRIENINGERs singen, einfach und ergreifend, wie alte Kirchenlieder. Das Lamm aus der Geheimen Offenbarung behielt Pater ROSNER jedoch bei, ohne Christus am Schluß nochmals zu zeigen.

Wenn man sich des näheren in seine Passion vertieft, dann fällt einem auf, wie sehr er die Sprache gehoben hat, wie glatt das nunmehr geht, wie fein er die Personen einer Gruppe (z. B. der Apostel, des Hohen Rates) gegeneinander abhebt, für manchen eine langweilige Sache, aber für die gebildeten Zuschauer – und Oberammergau hatte sie 1750 anscheinend bereits – ein wahres Vergnügen, unüberbietbar von anderen Passionsspielen. Andererseits kam P. ROSNER auch dem einfachen Volk entgegen, indem er altgewohnte Andachtsbilder liebevoll herausarbeitete, z. B. die Urlaubsnehmung, das Vesperbild. Wenn jemand die tiefere Beziehung eines Vorbildes nicht gleich verstand, so gab ihm der Schutzgeist in Wort und Gesang die nötigen Hinweise, mitunter fast in Moritatenton. Selbstverständlich ist die »Eherne Schlange« wieder da, sogar in zwei ausführlichen Phasen: zunächst wie Moses sie aufrichtet, sodann wie die Kranken flehend die Hände zu ihr erheben.

Eine besondere Beachtung verdient die Sprache, die wohl noch bayerisch ist, aber doch keinem eigentlichen Dialekt zuzuschreiben. Sie ist gemeinbairisch, wie es den Münchener Anstrengungen entsprach, der vom protestantischen Norden immer mehr nach Süden vordringenden neuhochdeutschen Schriftsprache ein südliches Gewicht entgegenzusetzen. Als P. ROSNER 1759 bis 1775 (mit einer kurzen Unterbrechung) in Freising als Rhetorikprofessor wirkte, ließ er bereits 1764 eines seiner lateinischen Dramen auch in eige-

Father ROSNER's immediate source was however the amateur theatre which, in the prologue and musical interludes, sometimes showed individual scenes or continuous secondary plots from the Old Testament instead of the allegories. His motionless tableaux were uncommonly suited to the Baroque love of spectacle. At first he was satisfied with 18 prefiguration scenes (three of them in a "chorus", all three stanzas of a song which differed metrically from the others), but he seems to have increased them as early as 1760. In the printed programme for the 1770 performance, which was banned, he has 23 prefiguration scenes. The nearby town of Tölz was insatiable and watched no less than 37 prefiguration scenes on Sundays in Lent and in Holy Week. The name for plays of this kind, "Passion through contemplation", also came from Tölz. The music has not survived, but six scenes (twice three) can be sung to two melodies by GRIENINGER simply and movingly, like old hymns. ROSNER retained the Lamb of the Revelation, but without showing Christ again at the end.

If we consider his Passion more closely we are struck by how much he improved the language, how smoothly it now flows, how well he contrasts the members of a group (e.g. the Apostles, the High Council) with each other. For some people it was tedious, but for the educated spectator–and evidently they were already to be found in Oberammergau in 1750–a true pleasure, unsurpassed by other Passion plays. On the other hand ROSNER also catered for the taste of simple people by lovingly showing old-accustomed devotional scenes such as the leavetaking and the Pieta. If someone did not understand immediately the deeper meaning of a prefiguration scene, the Tutelary Spirit gave him the necessary information in word and song, sometimes almost in the manner of a street ballad. Naturally the "brazen serpent" appears again, and even in two comprehensive episodes: firstly when Moses sets it up and then when the sick raise their hands to it in supplication.

The language, which is certainly still Bavarian but cannot be assigned to a true dialect, deserves special attention. It is common Bavarian, in conformity with Munich's efforts to impart a southern emphasis to the modern German literary language which was advancing further and further southwards from the Protestant North. While Father ROSNER was working as a teacher of rhetoric in Freising from 1759 to 1775 (with a brief interruption) he had one of his Latin dramas printed in his own

ner neuhochdeutscher Übersetzung drucken, das erste neuhochdeutsche Drama auf bayerischem Boden. Seine Passio nova zeigt ihn auf dem Weg dorthin, weithin in Bayern nachgespielt.

P. ROSNER hat 1749 das Passionsspiel nicht auf einen Satz geschrieben, sondern sozusagen in drei Lieferungen: zuerst den Sprechtext der als »Abhandlungen« bezeichneten 9 Akte, dann die Alexandriner und Liedstrophen des Schutzgeistes zu den »Betrachtungen« und schließlich szenische Anweisungen zur Erstellung der Vorbilder. In dieser Reihenfolge (vorausgeschickt den Text einer sonst nicht erhaltenen Perioche) hat sie ERLBÖCK in ein eigenes Buch zusammengeschrieben. Als ROSNER 1752/53 sich selbst einen Text anfertigte, hat er die richtige Reihenfolge zugrundegelegt, sich aber einmal geirrt, so daß er drei Szenenanweisungen zu einer »Betrachtung« gesammelt nachholen mußte. Auf dem Titelblatt machte er den Autorenvermerk in seiner gewohnten Abkürzung; die Auflösung stammt von seinem Freisinger Schüler und Theaterspieler FRANZ HOHENEICHER (1758 bis 1844): *P. Ferdinand ROSNER Benediktiner zu Ettal ein seiner Zeit berühmter Comicus.* Er wußte noch, daß ein »Comicus« kein Komiker war, sondern ein Theaterpater.

Für 1760 scheint P. ROSNER eine Erweiterung und vor allem eine Vermehrung der Vorbilder vorgenommen zu haben. Wir schließen dies aus der Übernahme dieses Textes in anderen Passionsorten wie z. B. 1762 in Tölz, desgleichen aus der gedruckt vorliegenden Perioche für das Passionsspiel 1770. Oberammergau hatte bereits 4000 Exemplare drucken lassen, da kam wie ein Blitz aus heiterem Himmel das Generalverbot sämtlicher Passionsspiele durch den kurfürstlichen Geistlichen Rat in München heraus. Eine Flut von Bittschriften ergoß sich über München, aber alle wurden unnachsichtlich abgewiesen, auch das der Oberammergauer. Aber diese gaben nicht so rasch auf, sondern schickten eine Deputation nach München. Sie wiesen in einer direkten Eingabe an den Kurfürsten darauf hin, daß ihr Passionsspiel »eine landtkündige sache sei und sie erforderlichen fahls mit viellen Tausend Zeugnissen bestärken können«, daß ihr Spiel nie Mißbräuche enthalten habe und sie als weitgereiste Männer »keine lächerlich, kündisch und abgeschmackte Evolutionen oder Personagen duldeten«, und daß eben deswegen ihre Passion »dergestalten berühmt geworden, das von 20, 30 und noch mehr Meill Weegs, als auch Bayern, Tyroll, Schwaben und dem Reich, item aus den Städten München, Freysing, Landshut, Innspruckh, Augspurg und anderen orthen nicht nur

modern German translation in 1764, the first modern German drama on Bavarian soil. His Passio Nova, widely performed in Bavaria, shows him on that path.

ROSNER did not write the Passion Play in 1749 all at once but in three instalments, so to speak: first, the spoken text of the nine acts, described as *"discourses"*, then the Alexandrines and song verses of the Tutelary Spirit for the *"contemplations"* and, finally, stage directions for the production of the prefiguration scenes. In this sequence (presumably the text of a programme which has not otherwise survived) ERLBÖCK wrote them together in a book of his own. When ROSNER prepared a text for himself in 1752/53, he used the correct sequence but made one mistake, so that he had to write down together three stage directions which he had missed out for a *"contemplation"*. On the title page he wrote the author's name and description in the customary abbreviated form: *"Father Ferdinand ROSNER, Benedictine of Ettal, a famous Comicus of his time."* The solution was given by his pupil in Freising, the actor FRANZ HOHENEICHER (1758–1844): he remembered that a *"Comicus"* was not a comic actor, but a monk, who was responsible for managing an amateur theatre.

For 1760 ROSNER seems to have expanded and, above all, added to the prefiguration scenes. This may be inferred from the adoption of the text in other places where Passion plays were given, e.g. in Tölz in 1762, and also from the printed programme for the 1770 Passion Play. Oberammergau had already had 4,000 copies printed when, like a bolt from the blue, the general prohibition of all Passion plays was ordered by the Prince Elector's Ecclesiastical Council in Munich, which was flooded with petitions as a result. However, they were all refused unrelentingly, even that from Oberammergau. Nevertheless the villagers did not give up so quickly, and they sent a deputation to Munich. In a direct petition to the Prince Elector they pointed out that their Passion Play was *"a thing well-known in the country, which can be supported by the testimony of many thousands if necessary"*, that their Play had never contained any abuses and that they, as well travelled people, did not *"tolerate ridiculous, childish and tasteless gestures or characters"*, and that precisely for this reason their Passion *"had become so famous that not only simple townspeople and country folk, but also persons of noble rank and learned persons hasten here from 20, 30 and more miles distant, and also from Bavaria, Tyrol, Swabia and the Empire, as well as from the towns of Munich, Freising, Landshut,*

einfältige Burgers- und Paursleuthe, sondern auch in Adelichen Characteurs stehende und Gelehrte Personen anhero eilen.« Am 17.5. hatten sie dies vorgetragen, am 4. 6. war Pfingstmontag, am 22.5. erhielten sie auf dem Amtsweg über den Ettaler Richter in Murnau die endgültige Ablehnung zugestellt. *»Wir fügten uns: und ließen die Aufführung bey seite«* betonen sie zehn Jahre später. Es muß ein trauriger Tag gewesen sein, als die Erfüllung des Gelübdes zum ersten Male ausfiel.

Am Ende des Jahres 1777 starb die Münchener Linie der Wittelsbacher aus. Kurfürst KARL THEODOR von der Pfalz, bisher schon ein Förderer der berühmten Mannheimer Musikschule und eines mutigen Nationaltheaters trat in München die Nachfolge an; er handhabe die Verordnung seines Vorgängers gegen die geistlichen Volksschauspiele weniger scharf, und so schöpften auch die Oberammergauer neue Hoffnungen. Zwar war P. ROSNER 1778 gestorben, aber in dem 1747 in Reutte geborenen Ettaler Pater MAGNUS KNIPFELBERGER besaß Ettal einen geeigneten Nachwuchs. In seinen Adern floß insofern Künstlerblut, als er mütterlicherseits aus der berühmten Malerfamilie ZEILLER stammte. Er kam 1755 ins Ettaler Seminar und kannte P. ROSNER noch persönlich. 1786 führte er ROSNERs *»Sächsischen Prinzenraub«* in neuhochdeutscher Sprache auf und wurde 1788 ans Freisinger Lyzeum berufen, wo er 1791/94 als Rhetorikprofessor auch das Theater betreute. Nach Ettal zurückgekehrt, lehrte er am dortigen Seminar wieder Rhetorik. Nach der Säkularisation wirkte er zunächst 1803/05 in Stötten als Hilfspriester, zog sich aber dann wegen zunehmender Altersgebrechlichkeit nach Schongau zurück, wo er anno 1825 verstarb. Sein Nachlaß ist leider verschollen. Erhalten hat sich jedoch in Oberammergau seine Bearbeitung der ROSNERschen Passion: Damit hat Oberammergau am 7. 1. 1780 *»anstatt dem Generalmandatmäßig interdizierten Passion ein anderes Spiel, das alt und Neue Testament betitelt, in dem für uns leidenden Gottmenschen zur Betrachtung vorgestellt, das von allen anstoßlichen Ungebührlichkeiten vollkommen gereingt sein,«* vorgelegt. Die Zensurbehörde war zufrieden und erteilte wenigstens ein Aufführungsprivileg. Nun möchte man meinen, sie hätten wirklich ein neues Stück vorgelegt, aber nein: über die Hälfte des Spieltextes stammte von ROSNER, sogar die meisten Alexandriner. Die Teufel wurden in eigene Opernszenen verbannt, die Allegorien stark zurückgedrängt. Dagegen rückten die Vorbilder aus dem Alten Testament mehr in den Vordergrund,

Innsbruck, Augsburg and other places." They presented their submissions on 17th May, 4th June being Whit Monday, and on 22nd May they received notice of a final refusal through the official channel of the Ettal judge in Murnau. *"We submitted: and left the performance aside",* they emphasised ten years later. It must have been a sad day when, for the first time, it was not possible to fulfill the vow.

At the end of 1777 the Munich line of the Wittelsbach family died out. The succession in Munich passed to Prince Elector KARL THEODOR of the Palatinate, a patron of the famous Mannheim school of music and a spirited national theatre. He applied his predecessor's degree against religious folk plays less strictly, with the result that the villagers of Oberammergau were given fresh hope. ROSNER died in 1778, but in Father MAGNUS KNIPFELBERGER, born in Reutte in 1747, Ettal possessed a suitable successor. He had artistic blood in his veins because on his mother's side he descended from the famous ZEILLER family of painters. He entered the Ettal Seminary in 1755 and knew ROSNER personally. In 1786 he produced ROSNER's *Kidnapping of the Saxon Prince"* in modern German and was appointed to the grammar school of Freising in 1788, where he also looked after the theatre as teacher of rhetoric from 1791 to 1794. After returning to Ettal he again taught rhetoric at the Seminary. After the secularisation he·at first acted as a vicar in Stötten in 1803/05, but then retired to Schongau because of increasing infirmity and died there in 1825. His writings have not survived. However, his adaptation of ROSNER's Passion has survived in Oberammergau. This means that on 7th January 1780 the village submitted, *"instead of the Passion prohibited by the general decree, another play entitled 'The Old and New Testament', presented for contemplation by us, suffering God-men, and which is completely purged of all objectionable and unseemly matter".* The censors were satisfied and at least granted a privilege of performance. It might be thought that a new play really had been submitted, but no: over half of the acting text originated from ROSNER as well as most of the Alexandrines. The devils were relegated to their own scenes with music, the allegories thrust into the background. On the other hand the prefiguration scenes from the Old Testament were given more emphasis since they of course had to bear the main burden of the new title.

Once again in 1790 the Play was given in Oberammergau by right, five times in succession. For the first

hatten sie doch die Hauptlast des neuen Titels zu tragen.

1790 spielte man in Oberammergau wieder gemäß Privileg, gleich fünfmal. Erstmals warb man in der Presse. Die Münchener Intelligenzblätter brachten am 21.5. einen Artikel »Über Religionsvorstellungen«. Nach einer allgemeinen Betrachtung über das Interesse des Staates an einer gewissen Religiosität der Untertanen hieß es: »*So wird alle Jahrzend in Amergau in Oberbaiern bey einer zahllos versammelten neuisraelitischen Menge Volks die Passionsvorstellung auf öffentlichem Platz vorgestellt. – Die Handlung fängt sich mit dem Rath der Christusverfolger an, und endet mit dieser Verderben. Das war's, würde Klopstock sagen, wonach ich zwanzig Jahre den Messias gearbeitet. – Wie getröstet und fähig zu allen guten Tathen muß jeder Waller hinweggehen der sagen kann: Ich habe gesehen die Thräne des Christen rinnen.*« Welcher Großmut der Zensur!

1799 starb Kurfürst KARL THEODOR, zwar von den Münchnern nicht geliebt, aber doch dem Volksempfinden näherstehend als sein Nachfolger MAXIMILIAN JOSEPH aus einer pfälzischen Nebenlinie. 1800 und 1801 konnte Oberammergau nochmals spielen, wenn auch durch den Krieg behindert, aber dann erklärte der allmächtige Minister MONTGELAS am 11. 9. 1801 das Oberammergauer Privilegium als erloschen. Im Jahre 1803 wurde auch das Kloster Ettal aufgrund des Reichsdeputationshauptbeschlusses aufgehoben.

Reise zu den Passionsspielen (1860/70)

time there was publicity in the press. On 21st May the Munich "Intelligenzblätter" published an article "On Religious Plays". After considering generally the State's interest in seeing that its subjects were to some extent religious, it says: "*Thus every ten years in Ammergau in Upper Bavaria the Passion Play is performed in a public square before a countless number of assembled New Israelites.–The action begins with the council of Christ's persecutors and ends with their undoing. That, Klopstock would have said, is what I spent twenty years writing 'The Messiah' for. How comforted and capable of every good deed must every pilgrim feel who, on leaving the place, can say: I have seen the Christians' tears flow.*" How generous of the censors!

In 1799 the Prince Elector KARL THEODOR died, unloved by the people of Munich but closer to national feeling than his successor, MAXIMILIAN JOSEPH, who came from a collateral line of the family in the Palatinate. In 1800 and 1801 Oberammergau gave the Play again, though hampered by the war, but then on 11th September 1801 the allpowerful Minister MONTGELAS declared Oberammergau's privilege extinguished. In 1803 the Monastery of Ettal was dissolved by virtue of the principal resolution of the Imperial Deputation.

DIE PROSAPASSION VON PATER OTHMAR WEIS

THE PROSE PASSION BY FATHER OTHMAR WEIS

Inzwischen hatte die neuhochdeutsche Schriftsprache auch in Süddeutschland auf breiter Front gesiegt; gereimte Verse galten übrigens im Schauspiel als »alter Zopf«, so daß selbst SCHILLER 1789 im Prolog zu »Wallensteins Lager« um Nachsicht bitten mußte, wenn die Sprache »ihr altes deutsches Recht, des Reimes Spiel, bescheiden wieder fordert«. An diesen Tatsachen konnte auch eine Reform des Oberammergauer Passionsspieles nicht vorübergehen. Wer aber konnte sie leisten, ohne daß die bisherige Entwicklung zerstört wurde?

Von den 1803 in Ettal zurückgebliebenen Patres, die ihre bescheidene Pension von 1 Gulden pro Tag verzehrten und auf den Tod oder ein neues Wirkungsfeld warteten, war sicher P. OTHMAR WEIS einer der rührigsten, denn er erteilte in dem ehemals Ettalischen Dorf Oberau im Loisachtal kostenlosen Elementarunterricht; er selbst war als Bauernsohn in dem Ettalischen Dorf Bayersoien 1769 auf die Welt gekommen. Da er sich als Meßdiener in Ettal geschickt zeigte, durfte er am dortigen Seminar die Studien beginnen. Nach ihrer Vollendung in München trat er 1790 in das Kloster

Pater Dr. Othmar Weis (1769–1843)

In the meantime the modern German literary language had won the day in South Germany also. Moreover, rhyming verses in drama were considered an *"antiquated custom"* so that even SCHILLER had to ask for indulgence in the prologue to *"Wallensteins Lager"* in 1789, if the language *"humbly demands again its old German right, the play of rhyme"*. No reform of the Oberammergau Passion Play could disregard these facts either. But who could accomplish it without destroying what had already been achieved?

Of the monks who had stayed in Ettal in 1803, spending their modest pension of 1 gulden a day while waiting for death or a new field of activity, Father OTHMAR WEIS was undoubtedly one of the most enterprising because he gave free elementary education in the village of Oberau in the Loisach valley, which had previously belonged to Ettal. He himself was born the son of a peasant in 1769 in the village of Bayersoien, which had also belonged to Ettal.

As he showed himself a skilful server at Mass in Ettal he was allowed to begin his studies in the

Ettal ein. Philosophie und Theologie studierte er in Ingolstadt, wohin er nach der Priesterweihe 1795 als Lehrer der 2. Grammatikklasse im Gymnasium zurückkehrte; zugleich immatrikulierte er sich an der Universität aufs neue, so daß er 1798 als Lehrer in die 3. Grammatikklasse vorrückte und zugleich am 15. 11. zum Dr. phil. promoviert wurde. Dann unterrichtete er im nächsten Schuljahr in der 2. Rhetorikklasse, die früher »Poesie« geheißen hatte. Wenn wir auch kein Theaterstück von ihm nennen können, so ist es doch gut, auch bei ihm wie bei seinen Vorgängern zu zeigen, daß er aus der Welt des Schultheaters kam. Er kehrte aus dem unruhigen Ingolstadt nach Ettal zurück, das ihn als Pfarrvikar von Eschenlohe einsetzte. Bei der Säkularisation 1803 erhielt diese Pfarrei aber ein anderer Ettaler Pater, und P. WEIS mußte als einer der Jüngsten bis 1812 warten, bis er in Jesenwang bei Fürstenfeldbruck eine eigene Pfarrei erhielt. Dort starb er 1843 als der letzte Angehörige des alten Ettal; er hatte noch erlebt, daß König Ludwig I. den Benediktinerorden anno 1830 in Metten wiederherstellte.

1810 ging vorüber, ohne daß Oberammergau eine neue Spielerlaubnis erhalten hätte; da wandte es sich an den in Ettal weilenden P. WEIS. Ihm gelang es, durch die Vorlage einer Prosa-Passion für 1811 eine Aufführungserlaubnis zu bekommen. In der Perioche berief er sich auf »Calmet, Braun etc.« Dabei interessiert uns weniger der als aufgeklärter Exeget bekannte Calmet als vielmehr Braun, ein ehemaliger Benediktiner von Tegernsee, in Freising ROSNERs Kollege und Freund, später Chorherr an der Liebfrauenkirche in München und leidenschaftlicher Reformator der bayerischen Volksschule, Förderer jeder Art von neuhochdeutscher Dichtung, Herausgeber einer deutschen Bibelübersetzung seit 1788, die aber unvollendet blieb, da er 1792 starb. Gerade er war es gewesen, der 1770 das allgemeine Passionsspielverbot erwirkte und eisern durchsetzte. O Ironie des Schicksals! Jetzt mußte er dem schlauen P. WEIS als Deckmantel für die Wiederbelebung Oberammergaus dienen!

Der Übergang zur Prosa bot P. WEIS die willkommene Gelegenheit, Bibelworte unmittelbar in den Handlungstext zu übernehmen, desgleichen die Reden des Chorführers statt in Alexandrinern nunmehr in Prosa ohne den Zwang eines Versmaßes zu gießen, nicht selten im Stil eines leidenschaftlichen Predigttones, der noch an »Sturm und Drang« erinnert. Alle Teufel und Allegorien sind von der Bühne verbannt; die Bühne ist wieder dreiteilig. Der neue Titel »Das große Opfer

seminary there. After completing them in Munich he entered the Monastery of Ettal in 1790. He studied philosophy and theology in Ingolstadt, returning there as a teacher of the 2nd grammar class in the grammar school after ordination in 1795. He immediately re-enrolled at the university so that in 1798 he was promoted to teach the 3rd grammar class and, on 15th November of the same year, gained his doctorate of philosophy. In the following school year he taught in the 2nd rhetoric class, which had previously been called "Poetry". Although we know of no plays by him it is right to point out that, like his predecessors, he came from the world of the amateur theatre. From Ingolstadt he returned to Ettal, which appointed him curate of Eschenlohe. However, on the secularisation in 1803 this parish received another monk from Ettal and WEIS, as one of the youngest, had to wait until 1812 before he was given his own parish of Jesenwang near Fürstenfeldbruck. He died there, the last member of old Ettal, but not before King Ludwig I restored the Benedictine Order in 1830 in Metten.

1810 passed by without Oberammergau obtaining a new licence for the Play, so it sought assistance from WEIS who was in Ettal at that time. He succeeded in obtaining a performing licence for 1811 by submitting a prose Passion. In the programme he cited the names of Calmet and Braun. In this context the reference to Calmet, an enlightened exegete of the Bible, is of less interest than the mention of Braun, a former Benedictine monk from Tegernsee, who was ROSNER's colleague and friend in Freising and later a canon in the Liebfrauenkirche in Munich. He was a passionate reformer of Bavarian primary schools and encouraged every kind of writing in modern German, also beginning the publication of a German translation of the Bible in 1788 which was not completed because he died in 1792. It was he who had procured and strictly enforced the general prohibition of Passion plays in 1770. It was an irony of fate that his name should now be used by the shrewd WEIS as a cover for the complete revival of Oberammergau.

The transition to prose offered WEIS the welcome opportunity to take words direct from the Bible into the text of the action and likewise to cast the speeches by the leader of the chorus in prose instead of Alexandrines and without the constraint of a fixed metre, often in the manner of an impassioned sermonising style reminiscent of "Sturm und Drang". Devils and allegories are all banished from the

auf Golgatha« stellt wieder Christus in die Mitte, kann aber nicht darüber hinwegtäuschen, daß das alte Spiel zugrundeliegt. Vor allem bleiben die Vorbilder, ja sie erhalten eine eigene, sozusagen maßgeschneiderte Musik. Der Lehrer ROCHUS DEDLER, ein geborener Oberammergauer und musikalisch sehr begabt, steuerte eine neue Musik bei, die dem Kammerorchester und dem Doppelquartett des Chores mit seinen Solisten würdige Aufgaben stellte, wie sie landauf, landab ein gutgeschulter Kirchenchor zu leisten hatte. Die Zensur hatte nichts einzuwenden, als den Oberammergauern durch die Vermittlung des Kronprinzenerziehers SAMBUGA 1811 die Erlaubnis erteilt wurde, das 1810 ausgefallene Gelübdespiel nachzuholen.

Es hatte sicher wiederum geeilt, denn als 1815 aus finanziellen und patriotischen Gründen eine Wiederholung des Spieles gestattet wurde, benützte WEIS trotz seiner Übersiedlung nach Jesenwang die Gelegenheit, gemäß dem neuen Titel »Jesus Messias oder die Menschenerlösung« den Anfang mit einem Bild »Vertreibung Adams und Evas nach dem Sündenfall aus dem Paradies« zu machen, zugleich mit der Verheißung der Erlösung. An den Anfang des eigentlichen Spieles setzte er eine ungemein wirksame Szene »Der Einzug in Jerusalem«.

Auch DEDLER ergänzte seine Musik entsprechend der neuen Vorlage sehr geschickt. Mit der Aufhebung des Klosters Ettal hatten sich in Oberammergau auch die Besitzverhältnisse geändert, indem die bisherigen 44 Ettalischen Lehen nunmehr gekauft oder ersteigert werden konnten. Bald konnte auch die Gemeinde eine größere Wiese kaufen und das Passionsspiel vom Friedhof weg auf diese Passionswiese verlegen, wo alsbald ein großer Stadel nicht nur als Bühnenhaus, sondern in den Zwischenjahren auch als Aufbewahrungsstätte der Requisiten diente. Ein 1762 in Oberammergau geborener und in Ettal als Singknabe ausgebildeter Geistlicher NIKOLAUS UNHOCH, 1833 als Pfarrer von Garmisch gestorben, zuvor aber Frühmesser in Oberammergau, baute bereits 1820 für den Friedhof eine neue Bühne und erweiterte sie 1830 für die Wiese, was nicht ganz ohne Kritik hingenommen wurde, sich aber dann durchgesetzt hat. Sie zeigt das mittlere, eigentliche Theater, flankiert von zwei Gebäudeteilen mit Tor und Veranda darüber (links das Haus des Pilatus, rechts das des Hohepriesters Kaiphas oder Annas) und je zwei Auftrittsmöglichkeiten aus der Tiefe und von der Seite. Bezeichnend für die Stärke der Tradition ist dabei die Tatsache, daß die Leidenswerkzeuge Christi, die

stage, which is once again divided into three. The new title, "The Great Sacrifice on Golgotha", puts Christ back in the centre of the action, but cannot conceal the fact that its basis is the old Play.

Above all, the prefiguration scenes remain, indeed they are given their own specially composed music. The teacher ROCHUS DEDLER, who was born in Oberammergau and had great musical talent, contributed new music which was a fitting task for the chamber orchestra and double quartet of the choir and soloists, a task which well trained church choirs far and wide had to perform. The censors had no objection when the villagers of Oberammergau were given a licence in 1811, through the good offices of SAMBUGA, the Crown Prince's tutor, to perform the Play which had not been given in 1810. Again there was certainly no time to lose when a repeat performance of the Play was allowed in 1815 on financial and patriotic grounds, because WEIS took the opportunity, in spite of having moved to Jesenwang, to open with the scene called "Expulsion of Adam and Eve from Paradise after the Fall" together with the promise of salvation, in accordance with the new title „Jesus the Messiah or the Salvation of Mankind". At the beginning of the Play itself he placed an extremely effective scene,

"The Entry into Jerusalem". DEDLER also composed additional music which met the new requirements very skilfully. The dissolution of the Monastery of Ettal had also brought about changes in the ownership of land in Oberammergau because the 44 benefices previously belonging to Ettal had now been sold or auctioned. Soon the parish also bought a large meadow, to which the Passion Play was moved from the churchyard. A large barn in the meadow was immediately put into use not only as a stage but also for storing props in the intervening years. In 1820 a new stage was built for the churchyard by NIKOLAUS UNHOCH, a clergyman who was born in Oberammergau in 1762 and was trained as a choirboy in Ettal. He later became the priest officiating at first morning Mass in Oberammergau and was parish priest of Garmisch when he died in 1833. In 1830 he extended the existing stage for the meadow, which gave rise to some criticism but was finally accepted. It has the actual stage in the centre flanked by two structures with a gate and veranda above (on the left Pilate's house, on the right that of the High Priest Caiaphas or Annas), each with two entrances from the back and the side. It is characteristic of the strength of the tradition that the instruments of Christ's suffer-

den nunmehr singenden und agierenden Chor behindern würden, den Engeln auf den seitlichen arkadenartigen Begrenzungen in die Hände gegeben sind.

In dieser neuen Kombination von Wort, Musik und Spielplatz erreichte Oberammergau im 19. Jahrhundert rasch wieder eine Höhe, die nicht nur MONTGELAS tolerierte, sondern auch andere Passionsorte veranlaßte, Oberammergau nachzuahmen. Inzwischen wuchs die Besucherzahl, damit auch die Notwendigkeit, Platz zu schaffen und den höheren Herrschaften Schutz vor Regen zu bieten. Das bedingte wiederum eine Verstärkung des Chores und des Orchesters, wobei man auch die Musik in das Prinzip der Entwicklung einbezog und z. B. zu lauten Blechinstrumenten griff. Die nunmehr einsetzende und 1850 von DEUTINGER veröffentlichte Berichterstattung war überwiegend positiv; nur die sprachliche Form empfand man allgemein als verbesserungsbedürftig.

Da schenkte die Vorsehung dem Dorf wieder den richtigen Mann: ALOIS DAISENBERGER. Auch er war als Bauernsohn und Ettaler Untertan in Oberau geboren (1799) und gehörte zu jenen Kindern, die P. OTHMAR WEIS nach 1803 unterrichtete, wofür er ihm zeitlebens dankbar blieb. Nach Studien in München und Landshut wurde er

Rochus Dedler (1779–1822)

ing, which would impede the choir which now sang and acted, were handed to the angels on the arcades at the far sides.

In this new combination of words, music and acting area Oberammergau again soon achieved a level in the 19th century which was tolerated not only by MONTGELAS but also caused other places with Passion plays to imitate Oberammergau.

In the meantime the number of visitors increased and, with it, the need to create more space and provide shelter from rain for high-ranking ladies and gentlemen. This in turn resulted in a strengthening of the choir and orchestra, the principle of development being applied to the music also and, for example, loud brass instruments being used for the first time. The regular report which now began and was published by DEUTINGER in 1850 was mainly positive; only the linguistic form was generally found to need more improvement. Once again Providence gave the village the right man: ALOIS DAISENBERGER. He also was born the son of a peasant under Ettal's rule in Oberau in 1799 and was one of the children taught by Father OTHMAR WEIS from 1803, for which he was grateful to WEIS throughout his life. After studying in Munich and Landshut he became a secular priest of the diocese of

1821 Weltgeistlicher der Diözese München; seine Sehnsucht war, einmal Pfarrer von Oberammergau zu werden, aber zunächst wurde er an verschiedenen Orten als Hilfsgeistlicher eingesetzt. 1844 empfahl er sich durch eine pietätvolle Lebensbeschreibung des 1843 verstorbenen P. WEIS. Endlich wurde er am 9. Juli 1845 auf besonderen Wunsch der Gemeinde zum Pfarrer von Oberammergau bestellt. Wie verschiedene Schauspiele aus seiner Feder bezeugen, fehlte es ihm nicht an Theaterverständnis; durch eine Übersetzung der »Antigone« des Sophokles bekundete er auch seine Verehrung der Antike. Auf vielfaches Drängen bereinigte er schon für 1850 einige Mängel des Textes, in größerem Ausmaß aber für 1860. Nunmehr ließ er den Chorführer in antiken Versmaßen sprechen. Er kam damit einem Zug der Zeit entgegen. Schon 1820 war die Meinung aufgetaucht, in Oberammergau habe man den letzten Rest des antiken religiösen Freilichttheaters vor sich; die erste Hälfte des Jahrhunderts war ohnehin stark vom klassischen Epigonentum geprägt, wie das München Ludwigs I. zeigt. Gegenüber dem eigentlichen Spiel aber, diesem »Vermächtnis der altdeutschen Frömmigkeit«, wie DAISENBERGER es nannte, hegte er eine gewisse Scheu. Er änderte wenig, kürzte aber den letzten Teil (Auferstehung) stark. Es schwebte

Geistl. Rat Joseph Alois Daisenberger (1799–1883)

Munich in 1821. It was his ambition to become the parish priest of Oberammergau, but at first he was appointed curate at various places. In 1844 his reputation was enhanced by a reverent biography of Father WEIS, who had died in 1843. He was finally appointed parish priest of Oberammergau on 9th July 1845 at the special wish of the parish. Various plays from his pen show that he had a feeling for the theatre, and his translation of Sophocles' *"Antigone"* revealed his admiration of the antique world. In response to frequent requests he rectified some shortcomings in the text of the Passion Play for 1850 and did so again, but on a larger scale, for 1860. The speeches he now wrote for the leader of the chorus were in classical metres, in accordance with the spirit of the time. As early as 1820 the opinion had been put forward that Oberammergau was the last survival of the classical religious open-air theatre. The first half of the century was in any case strongly marked by classical imitations, as the Munich of Ludwig I shows. Faced with the Play itself however, this *"legacy of medieval German piety"*, as DAISENBERGER called it, he felt a certain awe. He altered little but considerably shortened the last part (Resurrection). He had in mind a completely revised text in the iambic pentameters

ihm eine gesamte Texterneuerung in den seit SCHILLER das Drama beherrschenden jambischen Pentametern vor. Es gehörte zu den schmerzlichen Erlebnissen seines Ruhestandes (1869–1883), daß die Oberammergauer diesen neuen Text für 1880 ablehnten, wie sie auch alle Versuche der geistlichen und weltlichen Obrigkeiten, das Spiel zu modernisieren, vereitelten. Immerhin mußte von Zeit zu Zeit die Bühne erneuert werden. Der Spielleiter für 1890, Schnitzschuldirektor LUDWIG LANG, ging insofern ebenfalls »mit der Zeit«, als er im Sinne des bekannten Meiniger Hoftheaters auf historische Treue in Bühnenbild und Kostüm bedacht war. Ein wesentlicher Fortschritt war es, daß er das »Haus« des Pilatus und sein Gegenstück vom Mitteltheater löste und in die äußeren Ecken verlegte. So entstand beim großen Volksauflauf vor Pilatus eine ungemein größere Bewegtheit der Volksmenge als zuvor und heute noch bei vielen anderen Passionsbühnen, wo sie in die dem Zuschauerauge weniger faßbare Tiefe der Bühne hineinagiert.

which had dominated the drama since SCHILLER. It was a painful experience during his retirement (1869–1883) when the villagers of Oberammergau refused this new text for 1880, in the same way that they frustrated every attempt by the ecclesiastical and secular authorities to modernise the Play. At least the stage had to be renovated from time to time. The producer for 1890, LUDWIG LANG, director of the woodcarving school, likewise followed the fashion of the period in that he was concerned with historical accuracy in scenery and costumes, on the lines of the famous Court Theatre of Meinigen. He made a considerable improvement by moving Pilate's "house" and its counterpart from the central stage to the outer corners. This resulted in much greater animation in the crowd of people before Pilate than previously and than is still the case in many other Passion plays, where the people's gestures are directed towards the back of the stage and are less visible to the spectator.

Blick vom Zuschauerraum auf die Bühne (1860/70)

PROBLEME DES 20. JAHRHUNDERTS

Die Jahrhundertwende brachte dem Dorf den Bahnanschluß, dem Passionstheater eine technisch und akustisch einwandfreie Überdachung des Zuschauerraumes und Ettal eine Wiederbesiedlung durch Benediktiner aus Scheyern.

Der 1. Weltkrieg erzwang eine Verlegung des 1920 treffenden Spieles auf 1922, wobei die Inflation jeden Gewinn vereitelte. Andererseits faßte gerade damals ein in Volksstücken bereits bewährter Spielleiter, der Bildhauer GEORG JOHANN LANG (Spielleiter der Passionsspiele von 1930, 1934, 1950 und 1960), den Entschluß, die Bühne und die Bühnenbilder zu erneuern. Diesen Anregungen wurde stattgegeben. LANG entwarf anstelle des historischen und formal überholten Bühnenhauses eine moderne und zeitlose, in sich zusammenhängende und gegliederte Baumasse mit einer waagrechten Dominante. Für das etwas herausragende Bühnenhaus wurden von ihm mit der Gesamtarchitektur harmonisierende Bühnenbilder geschaffen. Der fast auf ein halbes Hundert angewachsene Chor wurde in einheitliche graublaue Mäntel gehüllt, mußte auf jede individuelle Bewegung verzichten und durfte sich nur in der Mitte durch Rückwärtsgehen öffnen, wenn eines der lebenden Bilder zu zeigen war. Die großen Leistungen GEORG JOHANN LANGs prägten das Passionsspiel bis in die heutige Zeit. 1950 wurde Dedlers Musik überdies von dem in Oberammergau geborenen Professor EUGEN PAPST bereinigt und fachmannisch ergänzt, so daß auch hierin den Kritikern der Wind aus den Segeln genommen wurde, soweit sie höhere Anforderungen stellten. So blieb immer noch das Problem der Textreform.

Den entscheidenden Anstoß gab das II. Vatikanische Konzil, das am 28.10.1965 erklärte: »Obgleich die jüdischen Obrigkeiten mit ihren Anhängern auf den Tod Christi gedrungen haben, kann man doch die Ereignisse seines Leidens weder allen damals lebenden Juden ohne Unterschied noch den heutigen Juden zur Last legen. Gewiß ist die Kirche das neue Volk Gottes, trotzdem darf man die Juden nicht als von Gott verworfen oder verflucht darstellen, als wäre dies aus der Hl. Schrift zu folgern.«

Zahlreiche Anregungen für eine Textreform wurden geprüft. Es kam jedoch für 1970 zu keiner

PROBLEMS OF THE 20TH CENTURY

With the turn of the century the village acquired a railway connection, the auditorium of the Passion Theatre was given a roof designed to meet the technical and acoustic requirements, and Ettal was repopulated by Benedictines from Scheyern.

The First World War forced the 1920 play to be postponed to 1922, when all the profit was consumed by inflation. On the other hand this was the period when the sculptor GEORG JOHANN LANG, who was already an experienced producer of folk plays and was to produce the Passion Plays of 1930, 1934, 1950 and 1960, decided to refurbish the stage and scenery. Instead of the historically and formally outmoded theatre, LANG designed a modern yet timeless, coherent yet articulated structure with a dominant horizontal line. For the slightly projecting stage he created settings which harmonised with the general architecture. He refused to use artificial light and any distracting detail. The choir, which had grown to almost 50, was dressed in uniform greyish blue robes and had to refrain from any individual movement, except that they opened in the middle by walking backwards when a tableau vivant had to be shown. LANG's great achievements have influenced the Passion Play right up to the present day. Furthermore in 1950 Dedler's music was revised and additional sections were expertly composed by Professor EUGEN PAPST, who was born in Oberammergau, so that here again the wind was taken out of the critics' sails when they made greater demands. Consequently the problem of textual reform still remained.

The decisive impulse was given by the Second Vatican Council which on 28th October 1965 declared: *"Although the Jewish authorities and their supporters insisted on Christ's death, the events of His suffering cannot be blamed on all Jews living at that time, without distinction, or on today's Jews. Certainly the church is the new people of God, nevertheless the Jews should not be represented as rejected or cursed by God, as if this should be inferred from Holy Scripture."*

Several suggestions for reform of the text were considered. However, no substantial change was made in 1970. Afterwards there were considerable differences of opinion in

Einzug in Jerusalem (1860)

35

wesentlichen Änderung. Nachher gab es in Oberammergau erhebliche Meinungsverschiedenheiten über das Ausmaß der Reform. Eine engagierte Gruppe um den Schnitzschuldirektor HANS SCHWAIGHOFER griff eine Anregung CARL ORFFs auf, als Alternative zum Weis-Daisenberger-Text die *Passio Nova* P. Rosners zu spielen. Der Gemeinderat erlaubte diesen Versuch, der als Rosner-Probe 1977 mehrmals in SCHWAIGHOFERs Inszenierung gezeigt wurde und vor allem bei den Massenmedien großen Anklang fand. Trotzdem ergaben eine Bürgerbefragung und die nächste Gemeinderatswahl 1978 eine erhebliche Mehrheit für die Anhänger des alten Spieles, wobei nicht bloß Textfragen den Ausschlag gaben. Die naive Ansicht, bei ROSNER seien nicht die Juden an Christi Tod schuldig, sondern die höllischen Mächte – vom einzelnen Sünder abgesehen –, und man könnte durch Streichung aller judenfeindlichen Stellen bei ROSNER *das* Spiel für die Zukunft gewinnen, überzeugte nicht. Dazu kam, daß die verwendete Musik des Zeitgenossen und Kollegen Pater ROSNERs in Ettal, des »Mannheimers« FRANZ XAVER RICHTER, zu wuchtig und lang und überdies auf eine Vielzahl von auswärtigen Kräften angewiesen war. Den Höllenspuk und die Allegorien

betrachteten viele nur als interessante Folklore. Es sind trotzdem tiefe Eindrücke geblieben; entscheidend aber war die Meinung der einheimischen Bevölkerung. Auch für sie war nunmehr der Weis-Daisenberger-Text so nicht mehr im ganzen Wortlaut tragbar. Der gemäß dem Vatikanum gereinigte Text wurde dem Münchener Erzbischof, Kardinal RATZINGER, vorgelegt. Seine Billigung hat an Gewicht gewonnen, seit er als Präfekt der Glaubenskongregation an die Kurie in Rom berufen wurde. Es gelang dem neuen Spielleiter HANS MAIER in der Kürze der Zeit 1980 den überarbeiteten Text mit alten und neuen Mitteln zu einem erfolgreichen Spiel zu gestalten, das Spieler und Zuschauer davon überzeugte, daß eine Weiterentwicklung auf diesem Weg möglich ist, ohne daß das Oberammergauer Spiel seine Identität verliert. Am 5. Mai 1983 wurde der Text erneut von einer Abordnung der Gemeinde und von Vertretern der Arbeitsgruppe für Fragen des Judentums in der Ökumenekommission der Deutschen Bischofskonferenz durchbesprochen, verbessert und am Schluß einstimmig gebilligt. Im vorigen Jahrhundert hat einer geschrieben, wunderbarer als das Spiel sei seine Entstehung. Wir meinen, daß sein Fortleben durch 350 Jahre trotz so vieler äußerer und

Einzug in Jerusalem (1860)

Oberammergau regarding the extent of the reform. A committed group around HANS SCHWAIGHOFER, the director of the woodcarving school, took up CARL ORFF's suggestion that Father Rosner's *Passio Nova* should be performed as an alternative to the Weis-Daisenberger text.

The Parish Council permitted this experiment and Rosner's version was tried out in performance in SCHWAIGHOFER's production several times in 1977, receiving an enthusiastic response from the mass media above all. However, a referendum of the inhabitants and the next elections to the Parish

Council in 1978 produced a substantial majority for the supporters of the old Play, although the issue was not decided just by textual questions. People were not convinced by the naive view that ROSNER's text did not make the Jews guilty of Christ's death, for which the powers of Hell were responsible (apart from the individual sinner), and that the ideal version for the future would be obtained by the deletion of all passages hostile to the Jews in ROSNER's text. Furthermore the accompanying music by ROSNER's contemporary and colleague in Ettal, the *"Mannheimer"* FRANZ XAVER RICHTER,

Kreuzigung vom Theaterplatz aus (1890)

the Archbishop of Munich, Cardinal RATZINGER. His approval was given additional weight after he was appointed to the Roman Curia as Prefect of the Congregation.

In the short time up to 1980 the new producer, HANS MAIER, by using methods both old and new succeeded in making the revised text into a successful play which convinced actors and audience alike that further development along this path is possible without the Oberammergau Play losing its identity. On 5th May 1983 the text was once again discussed, amended and finally approved unanimously by a deputation from the Parish and representatives of the Working Group for Questions of Judaism of the Ecumenical Committee of the German Bishop's Conference.

In the previous century someone wrote that the origin of the Play was more miraculous than the Play itself. We believe that its continued existence for 350 years in spite of so many external and internal difficulties is even more miraculous, and in any case in this continuity it is unequalled anywhere in the world. We are confident that even in subsequent modifications it will always proclaim the same message as at the beginning:

Look up to the Cross! Then the Lord will heal you.

Kreuzigung (1860)

innerer Schwierigkeiten noch wunderbarer ist, jedenfalls in dieser Kontinuität einmalig auf der Welt. Wir haben das Vertrauen, daß es auch in neuen Wandlungen immer wieder das gleiche wie am Anfang verkünden wird:

Blickt auf zum Kreuz! Dann wird der Herr euch heilen.

was too weighty and long, and also required many performers from outside. The visions of Hell and the allegories were regarded by many only as interesting folklore. Although a deep impression was made, the issue was decided by the opinion of the local people.

However, they also no longer found the Weis-Daisenberger text acceptable in its entirety. After being revised in accordance with the recommendations of the Vatican Council it was submitted to

LITERATUR

LITERATURE

Da diese Einleitung bewußt knapp gehalten ist, wird der Leser, der ausführliche Darstellungen, Beweise und Belege, eventuell auch weiterführende Literatur sucht, auf folgende Publikationen des gleichen Autors verwiesen:

Das Passionsspiel von Oberammergau 1634–1950, Kunstverlag Ettal 1950.

Passionsspiele als Zeugen der sich wandelnden Frömmigkeit, in »Passionsspiele heute?« Meitingen-Freising 1973, S. 15–24.

Ferdinand Rosner, Passio Nova von 1750, historisch-kritische Ausgabe mit einem längeren Nachwort, Bern 1974.

Nie wieder: Verfluchte Synagoge! Die Rolle des Judentums in der Geschichte des Oberammergauer Passionsspieles, Schönere Heimat 1980, S. 288–292.

Die ersten hundert Jahre des Oberammergauer Passionsspieles, Jahrbuch für Volkskunde, Neue Folge V, Würzburg 1982, S. 78–125.

Ferdinand Rosner, Leben und Werke, München 1984.

Prolog (1870)

Since this introduction is intentionally brief, readers seeking detailed accounts and documentary information or further reading are referred to the following publications by the same author:

The Oberammergau Passion Play 1634–1950, Kunstverlag Ettal 1950.

Passion plays as testimony of changing piety, in "Passion plays today?", Meitingen-Freising 1973, pp. 15–24.

Ferdinand Rosner, Passio Nova of 1750, a critical historical edition with an epilogue, Berne 1974.

Never again: Accursed synagogue! The role of Judaism in the history of the Oberammergau Passion Play, Schönere Heimat 1980, pp. 288–292.

The first hundred years of the Oberammergau Passion Play, Folklore Yearbook, New Series V, Würzburg 1982, pp. 78–125.

Ferdinand Rosner, Life and Works, Munich 1983 and 1984.

PASSION

PROLOG
MIT CHOR

PASSIONSGELÜBDE
AM FRIEDHOF 1633

2

»O HEILIGES KREUZ
SEI UNS GEGRÜSST«

INZUG
N JERUSALEM.
ESUS WIRD
JBELND VOM
OLK BEGRÜSST

SEGNUNG
DER KRANKEN
UND KINDER

VERTREIBUNG DER
HÄNDLER AUS DEN
TEMPELHALLEN

DIE HOHEN PRIESTER
UND ÄLTESTEN

BETHANIEN,
ABSCHIEDSMAHL
UND
SALBUNG

DIE BRAUT
IM HOHEN LIEDE

4

JESU ABSCHIED
VON SEINER
MUTTER MARIA

UDAS MIT DEN
HÄNDLERN

MARIA
FELLNER THERESIA

NNA
UND TRAUBEN

5

FUSSWASCHUNG

ABENDMAHL

»DAS IST
MEIN BLUT«

JUDASBISSEN

»KINDER,
WAS SEID IHR
SO TRAURIG«

ABENDMAHLGEBET

DATHAN MIT JUDAS
VOR DEM
HOHEN RAT

JDAS ERHÄLT
IE 30 SILBERLINGE

NIKODEMUS
UND JOSEPH
VON ARIMATHÄA
VERLASSEN DEN RAT

CHRISTUS
AM ÖLBERG

JUDAS NAHT MIT
DER TEMPELWACHE

JDASKUSS

CHRISTUS
JABLONKA MAX

CHRISTUS
VOR ANNAS

FALSCHE ZEUGEN
VOR DEM
HOHEN RAT

JESUS VOR DEM
HOHEN RAT

BESCHLUSS DI
TODES JES

KAIN UND ABEL

11

JUDAS BEREUT
SEINE TAT

PETRUS
WIRD BEDRÄNGT

PETRUS VERLEUGNET
SEINEN MEISTER

DER DULDER JOB

12

VERSPOTTUNG

JESUS
VOR PONTIUS
PILATUS

JESUS
VOR HERODES
ANTIPAS

GEISSELUNG
AUF BEFEHL
VON PILATUS

DORNENKRÖNUNG

»ECCE HOMO«
CHRISTUS
ZWINK RUDOLF

JOSEPH'S TRIUMPH

13

CHRISTUS ERWARTET
SEIN URTEIL

JESUS
UND BARABBAS
VOR DEM VOLKE

LATUS WÄSCHT
EINE HÄNDE
N UNSCHULD

DIE VERURTEILUNG
JESU
ZUM KREUZESTOD

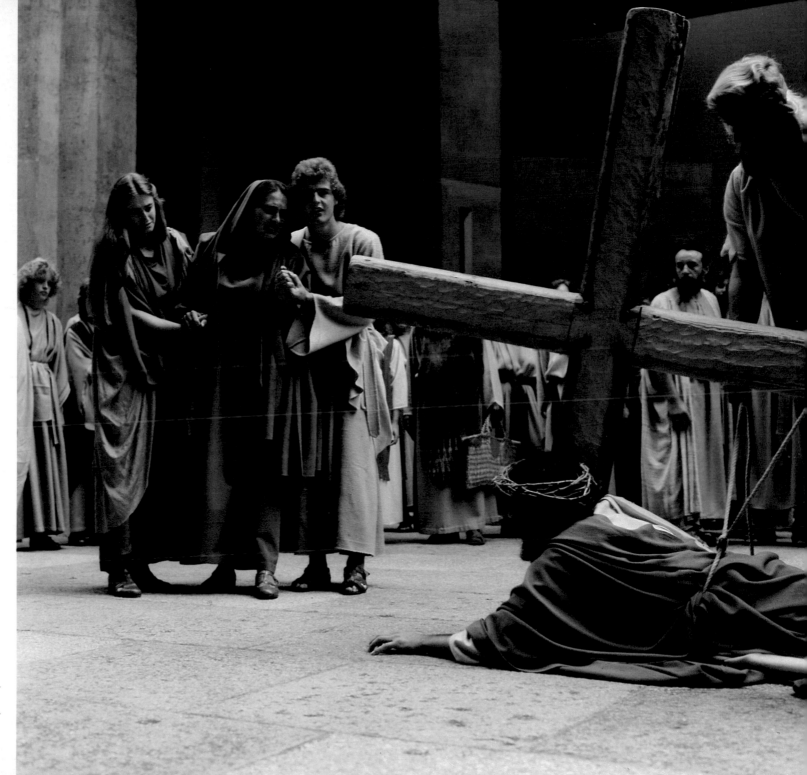

JESUS BEGEGNET
SEINER MUTTER

JESUS FÄLLT
UNTER DEM KREUZE

VERONIKA
BEGEGNET JESUS

IMON VON CYRENE
HILFT JESUS
DAS KREUZ TRAGEN

VERONIKA
REICHT JESUS
DAS SCHWEISSTUCH

CHRISTUS
AM KREUZE
ERHÖHT

KREUZIGUN

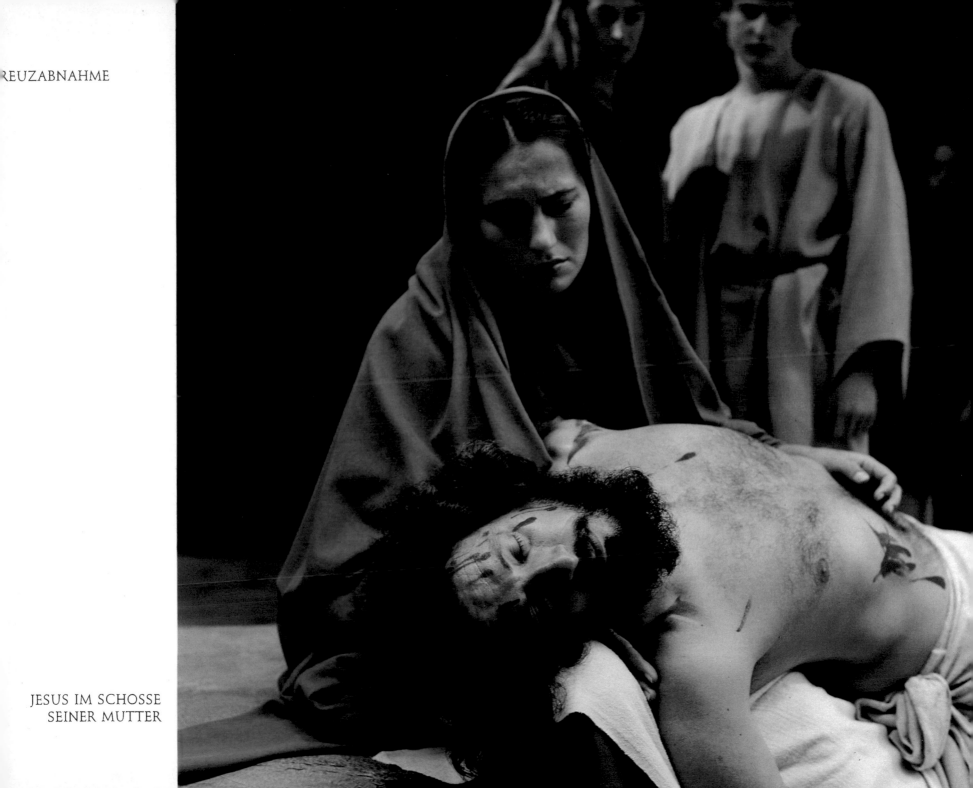

REUZABNAHME

JESUS IM SCHOSSE
SEINER MUTTER

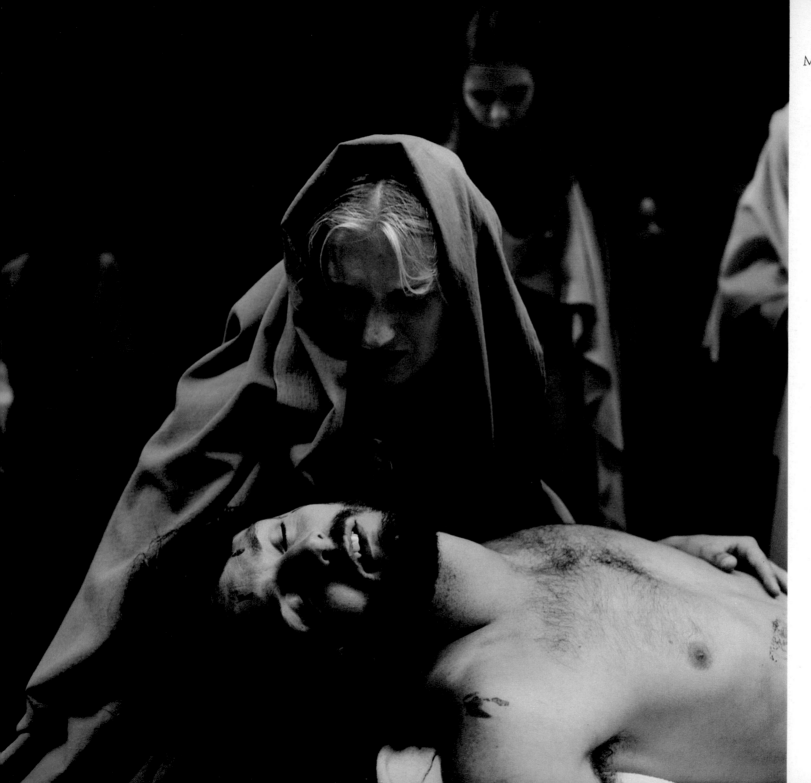

AUFERSTEHUN

DIE LEBENDEN
BILDER

THE TABLEAUX
VIVANTS

1 VERTREIBUNG AUS DEM PARADIESE

Das erste Menschenpaar sündigte durch Ungehorsam, da es eine Frucht von dem verbotenen Baume der Erkenntnis von Gut und Böse aß. Gott wies es aus dem Paradies und »*ließ östlich des Gartens Eden die Kerubim lagern und das lodernde Feuerschwert, damit sie den Weg zum Baum des Lebens bewachten*« (Gen. 3,24). Deshalb steht links in himmlischem Glanze ein Kerub mit dem Flammenschwert vor dem Eingang zum Paradies und weist Adam und Eva streng fort, desgleichen die verführerische Schlange. Eva, der ein besonders hartes Los als Frau vorausgesagt worden ist, blickt erschreckt und traurig zurück.

EXPULSION FROM PARADISE

The first two people on earth sinned by disobedience because they ate a fruit from the forbidden tree of the knowledge of good and evil. God sent them out of Paradise and *"at the east of the garden of Eden he placed the cherubim, and a flaming sword which turned every way, to guard the way to the tree of life"* (Genesis 3, 24). For this reason a cherub stands at the left in the splendour of heaven, holding a flaming sword at the entrance to Paradise and sternly pointing in another direction for Adam and Eve as well as the serpent of temptation. Eve, who has been told that she will have a particularly hard fate as a woman, looks back in fear and sadness.

2 PASSIONSGELÜBDE AM FRIEDHOF 1633

Als 1933 drei Jahrhunderte seit dem Passionsgelübde verflossen waren, schrieb LEO WEISMANTEL das Stück »*Die Pestnot anno 1633*«, das seither jedem Passionsjahr vorausgeschickt und im Spiel durch sein Schlußbild in Erinnerung gebracht wird. Wir sehen die Verehrung des aufgerichteten Kreuzes durch jung und alt, gesund und krank. Die erhobenen Hände deuten auf das Gelöbnis hin. Diese Szene findet vor der Mauer des Friedhofes statt, auf dem das gelobte heilige Spiel durch fast zwei Jahrhunderte über die Bretter ging, bis es 1830 auf die Passionswiese verlegt wurde, wo es bis zur Gegenwart verblieb.

CHURCHYARD VOW TO PERFORM THE PASSION PLAY, 1633

In 1933, to mark the 300th anniversary of the vow to perform the Passion Play, LEO WEISMANTEL wrote the play *"Die Pestnot anno 1633"* which has since preceded every Passion year and is brought to mind in the Passion Play by the final tableau. We see the adoration of the upright cross by young and old, healthy and sick. Their raised hands suggest the vow. This scene takes place in front of the wall of the churchyard in which the promised holy play was performed for almost 200 years until, in 1830, it was moved to the Passionswiese where it is still performed at our days.

3 TOBIAS' ABSCHIED

Der Abschied des jungen Tobias, der von seinem Vater in die Ferne geschickt wird, um eine hinterlegte Summe einzutreiben, dient hier als Parallele für die rührende Szene, als Jesus von seiner Mutter scheiden muß, um im Auftrag des ewigen Vaters die Schuld der Menschheit zu sühnen. Die Mutter des Tobias klagt dem Vater unter Tränen: »*Warum hast du ihn nur fortgeschickt?*« (Tob. 5,18). Schwer ist diese Stunde für ihr mütterliches Herz. Der Erzengel Raphael hat sich in Gestalt eines Jünglings als Begleiter angeboten; er drängt zum Aufbruch. In seine Richtung weist der Stab des knienden Tobias. Auch Jesus wird von einem Engel ermahnt, den Willen des Vaters zu erfüllen.

TOBIAS' FAREWELL

The farewell of the young Tobias, who is sent by his father to a distant part to collect a sum of money left in trust, is used here as a parallel to the touching scene in which Jesus has to leave his mother in order to atone for the guilt of mankind, at the bidding of the eternal Father. Tobias' mother complains tearfully to his father, *"Why have you sent our child away?"* (Tobit 5, 18). It is a difficult moment for her motherly heart. The archangel Raphael, in the form of a young man, offers to accompany Tobias and urges him to start his journey. Tobias is kneeling, while his staff points in the archangel's direction. Jesus also is exhorted by an angel to do his Father's will.

4 · DIE BRAUT IM HOHEN LIEDE

Die Braut aus dem Hohenlied Salomons ist kein historisches, sondern ein literarisches Vorbild. Dieses Lied ist zwar eine Sammlung von Liebesliedern, handelt aber nicht nur von sinnlichen, sondern auch von seelischen Beziehungen, was ihm erst einen tiefen religiösen Sinn gibt. Das Leid der verlassenen Gottesmutter Maria spiegelt sich wider: »Auf meinem Lager such' ich ihn, den meine Seele liebt.« Mitfühlende Gespielinnen trösten sie: »Wohin ist dein Geliebter gegangen, Schönste der Frauen? Wir wollen ihn suchen mit dir.« (Hoheslied 6,1). Aber die bangen Ahnungen Mariens trügen nicht. Am Kreuzweg wird sie ihren Sohn wiedersehen.

THE BRIDE IN THE SONG OF SOLOMON

The bride in the Song of Solomon is not a historical prefiguration but a literary one. Although this Song is a collection of love songs it is concerned not only with physical but also spiritual relationships, which really gives it a profound religious meaning. It mirrors the sorrow of the deserted Mother of God, Mary: "Upon my bed by night I sought him whom my soul loves." The bride's sympathetic companions console her: "Whither has your beloved gone, O fairest among women? Whither has your beloved turned, that we may seek him with you?" (Song of Solomon 6,1). But Mary's apprehension is not for nothing. She will see her Son again on the way of the cross.

5 · MANNA UND TRAUBEN

Jesus hat in bezug auf das Manna, das Moses in der Wüste regnen ließ (Exod. 16,14–18), betont: »Ich bin das Brot des Lebens; wer zu mir kommt, wird nicht mehr hungern, und wer an mich glaubt, wird nicht mehr dürsten.« (Joh. 6,35). Mit dem Mannaregen verbindet sich die Rückkehr der Kundschafter aus Kanaan, die als Beweis für die Fruchtbarkeit des versprochenen Landes vor allem eine riesige Traube brachten, Symbol der Gnadenfülle (Num. 13,26). Brot und Wein in das Fleisch und Blut Christi zu verwandeln, blieb bis heute die Aufgabe der Eucharistiefeier, die Jesus beim letzten Abendmahl eingesetzt hat.

MANNA AND GRAPES

Referring to the manna which Moses caused to rain down in the desert (Exodus 16, 14–18), Jesus said, "I am the bread of life; he who comes to me shall not hunger, and he who believes in me shall never thirst" (John 6, 35). The rain of manna is linked with the return of the scouts from Canaan who, as proof of the fertility of the promised land, brought a huge bunch of grapes, a symbol of the abundance of grace (Numbers 13, 26). To change bread and wine into the flesh and blood of Christ is still the purpose of the sacrament of the Eucharist which Jesus instituted at the last supper.

6 · JOSEPH'S VERKAUF

Joseph war der Lieblingssohn Jakobs, weil er ihm noch im hohen Alter geboren wurde; um so mehr haßten ihn seine älteren Brüder. Sie wollten ihn töten, doch Ruben, der älteste, warnte sie, Bruderblut zu vergießen, weshalb sie Joseph in eine trockene Zisterne warfen und alsbald an vorüberziehende Händler um 20 Silberlinge als Sklaven verkauften (Gen. 37,26). Joseph stieg später in Ägypten zum Vizekönig auf und bewahrte als solcher auch Vater und Brüder vor dem Hungertod. So wird auch der von Judas um den Preis eines Sklaven verkaufte Jesus erhöht werden und die Seinen vom Verderben erretten.

JOSEPH IS SOLD BY HIS BROTHERS

Joseph was Jacob's favourite son because he was born in his father's old age, and he was all the more hated by his older brothers. They wanted to kill him, but Reuben, the eldest, warned them against spilling a brother's blood, so they threw Joseph into a dry well and then sold him as a slave to some passing traders for 20 pieces of silver (Genesis 37, 26). Later Joseph rose to become governor of Egypt and, as such, saved his father and brothers from dying of starvation. In the same way Jesus, who was sold by Judas for the price of a slave, will be exalted and will save his people from damnation.

ADAM ARBEITET IM SCHWEISSE SEINES ANGESICHTS

Bei der Vertreibung aus dem Paradies hat Gott zu Adam gesagt: »*Deinetwegen ist der Ackerboden verflucht. Mit Schweiß im Gesicht wirst du dein Brot essen, bis du zurückkehrst zum Ackerboden. Von ihm bist du ja genommen, denn Staub bist du, und zum Staub kehrst du zurück.*« (Gen. 3,17–19). Wie schwer tut sich Adam mit seinem Holzpflug, obwohl Kain und Abel vorgespannt sind! Wie sehr ist Eva als Mutter vieler Kinder beansprucht! – Der bittere Schweiß Adams gilt als Vorbild für jenen blutigen Schweiß, der Jesus aus den Poren drang, als er am Ölberg den Kelch des Leidens mitsamt der Todesangst annahm.

JOAB TÖTET AMASA BEIM FREUNDSCHAFTSKUSS

König David hatte seinen Heerführer Joab abgesetzt und den Oberbefehl Amasa übertragen, aber noch bevor dieser seinen Posten antreten konnte, begegnete ihm Joab mit seinen Soldaten beim Stein von Gideon (bei den Felsen von Gabaon). Er heuchelte Freundschaft, faßte Amasas Bart, um ihn zu küssen, und durchbohrte ihn gleichzeitig mit dem heimlich gezückten Schwert, bevor die Soldaten eingreifen konnten (2. Sam. 20,10). – Abscheulicher als den Verrat des Judas empfand man immer die Art, w i e er seinen Meister überlieferte. »*Mit einem Kuß verrätst du den Menschensohn?*«

MICHÄAS EMPFÄNGT DEN LOHN DER WAHRHEIT

Als König Ahab von Israel den ihn besuchenden König Joschafat von Juda zum Krieg gegen Ramot-Gilead gewinnen wollte, ließ er durch seine von einem Lügengeist geblendeten Hofpropheten den Sieg vorhersagen. Einzig Micha (Michäas) sagte seinem König Niederlage und Tod voraus, wie es später eintrat. Doch damals schlug einer der falschen Propheten dem Micha ins Gesicht und rief: »*Wie sollte Gottes Geist von mir gewichen sein und mit dir reden?*« (1. Kön. 22,24) Achab ließ Micha gefangen abführen wie Annas Jesus, obwohl dieser geschlagen wurde, ohne daß man ihn einer Unwahrheit überführt hatte.

ADAM WORKS IN THE SWEAT OF HIS FACE

When God expelled Adam from Paradise he said to him, *"Cursed is the ground because of you . . . In the sweat of your face you shall eat bread till you return to the ground, for out of it you were taken; you are dust, and to dust you shall return"* (Genesis 3, 17–19). How hard Adam works with his wooden plough, even though Cain and Abel are harnessed to it! What heavy demands are made on Eve as the mother of many children! Adam's bitter sweat is seen as a prefiguration of the bloody sweat which poured from Jesus when, on the Mount of Olives, he accepted the cup of suffering and, with it, the fear of death.

JOAB KILLS AMASA WHEN KISSING HIM IN FRIENDSHIP

King David had removed Joab as leader of his army and given command to Amasa, but before Amasa could take up his post he was met by Joab and his soldiers at the rock of Gideon. Joab feigned friendship, took hold of Amasa's beard to kiss him and, at the same time, stabbed him with a sword which he had secretly drawn, before the soldiers could intervene (2 Samuel 20, 10). The way in which Judas handed over his master has always been found more repugnant than his actual betrayal. *"Would you betray the Son of man with a kiss?"*

MICAIAH RECEIVES HIS REWARD FOR TELLING THE TRUTH

When King Ahab of Israel tried to persuade King Jehoshaphat of Judah, who was visiting him, to join him in a war against Ramoth in Gilead, victory was prophesied for him by his court prophets, who had been blinded by a spirit of falsehood. Micaiah was the only one who foretold death and defeat for his king, which actually came about later. But when he foretold this, one of the false prophets struck him in the face and said, *„How did the Spirit of the Lord go from me to speak to you?"* (1 Kings 22, 24). Ahab had Micaiah arrested and taken away in the same way that Annas did Jesus, although Jesus was beaten without having been found guilty of telling an untruth.

NABOTH'S STEINIGUNG

Naboth verkaufte seinen ererbten Weinberg nicht um viel Geld an den König Ahab, so daß die Königin Isebel (Jezabel) einen Scheinprozeß veranlaßte, in dem zwei falsche Zeugen Naboth beschuldigten, er habe Gott und den König gelästert. Darauf stand Steinigung. Vom Hintergrund aus beobachtet die listige Königin, wie Naboth seinen Tod gefaßt erwartet. (1. Kön. 21,13) – Falsche Zeugen halfen mit, Jesus zum Tode zu verurteilen. Im Gleichnis von den bösen Winzern hatte er wenige Tage zuvor sein Recht auf den Weinberg seines himmlischen Vaters dargetan, das ihm auch der Tod nicht nehmen könne.

 KAIN UND ABEL

Der erste Tote auf Erden ist ein Ermordeter. *»Kain, wo ist dein Bruder Abel? Das Blut deines Bruders schreit zu mir vom Ackerboden.«* Kain bekennt schließlich: *»Zu groß ist meine Schuld, als daß man sie wegnehmen könnte.«* Er verzweifelt, jedoch Gott, der wiederholt sagt, daß er den Tod des Sünders nicht wolle, sondern daß er sich bekehre und lebe, macht ihm zum Schutz vor Blutrache ein Zeichen auf die Stirne (Gen. 4,15). – Judas erging es schlimmer als Kain, denn er verzweifelte auch an Gottes Güte und machte seinem Leben, nicht aber seiner Qual durch Selbstmord ein Ende.

 DER DULDER JOB

Das Buch Job gilt als der erste Versuch, durch Rede und Gegenrede zu ergründen, warum Gott auch den Gerechten versucht werden und leiden läßt. Satan darf mit Gottes Zulassung den schuldlosen Job aller Güter berauben und ihn sogar mit Aussatz heimsuchen, so daß sich Job in völligem Elend in die Asche setzt. Alle Reden seiner Frau und seiner Freunde können ihn nicht in seiner Gottergebenheit irremachen (Job. 2,12). Ähnlich wird Jesus von der Tempelwache verhöhnt und sogar körperlich gequält, ohne daß er klagt. Er schweigt.

THE STONING OF NABOTH

Naboth refused King Ahab's offer of a high price for the vineyard he had inherited. Queen Jezebel arranged a mock trial at which two false witnesses accused Naboth of cursing God and the king. The penalty for this was stoning to death. From a distance the crafty queen watched Naboth calmly awaiting his death (1 Kings 21, 13). False witnesses helped to condemn Jesus to death. In the parable of the wicked vine-growers he had, a few days previously, asserted his right to the vineyard of his heavenly Father, which even death could not take from him.

CAIN AND ABEL

The first man to die on earth was murdered. *"Cain, where is Abel your brother? The voice of your brother's blood is crying out to me from the ground."* Finally Cain confesses, *"My guilt is too great for it to be taken away,"* and he despairs. But God, who repeatedly says that he does not wish a sinner's death, but that he should mend his ways and live, put a mark on his brow to protect him from blood vengeance (Genesis 4, 15). It fared worse with Judas than Cain, because Judas even despaired of God's goodness and put an end to his life, but not to his torment, by suicide.

THE LONG-SUFFERING JOB

The book of Job is regarded as the first attempt to fathom, in the form of a dialogue, why God allows even the righteous to be tempted and to suffer. With God's permission, Satan is allowed to rob the innocent Job of all his goods and even afflict him with sores, so that Job sits in the ashes in utter misery. Nothing his wife or his friends say can make him lose his faith in God (Job 2, 12). In the same way Jesus is mocked by the guards of the temple and even physically tormented, without complaining. He says nothing.

JOSEPH'S TRIUMPH

Joseph wird aus dem Kerker geholt, und nach der Deutung der Pharao-Träume (sieben Jahre des Überflusses und sieben Hungerjahre) zum Vizekönig von Ägypten erhöht. Der Pharao selbst befiehlt, ihn dem jubelnden Volk im Triumphzug zu zeigen. (Gen. 41,42–44.) Auch Jesus wird aus dem Kerker vorgeführt und von Pilatus erhöht, aber am Kreuze, den Königstitel über seinem Haupte. Jesus sieht voraus, daß er seinem Volk Heil und Rettung in Ewigkeit erwirbt.

JOSEPH'S TRIUMPH

Joseph is taken from prison and, after interpreting Pharaoh's dreams (seven years of plenty and seven years of famine), he is raised in rank and appointed governor of Egypt. Pharaoh himself orders that Joseph be shown to the rejoicing people in a triumphal procession (Genesis 41, 42–44). Jesus also is taken from prison and shown to the people. He is raised up by Pilate, but on the cross, the title of "king" above his head. Jesus foresees that he will bring his people eternal grace and salvation.

 DIE AUSLOSUNG DES SÜNDENBOCKES

Wieder handelt es sich nicht um ein geschichtliches Bild, sondern um eine Gesetzesvorschrift für eine Zeremonie am Jom Kippur, dem Versöhnungstag. Der Hohepriester (Aaron) muß von zwei Böcken einen auslosen, der für die Sünden des Volkes als Opfer geschlachtet wird, während der andere, symbolisch mit den Freveltaten Israels beladen, in die Wüste geschickt wird, sozusagen dem Wüstendämon Asasel zur Beute (Lev. 16,7–10; 16,21–22). Ebenso soll das Volk zwischen Jesus und Barabbas wählen. Jesus wird als das Lamm Gottes die Sünde der Welt hinwegnehmen, während Barabbas ins Ungewisse und Dämonische davonziehen kann.

THE CHOOSING OF THE SCAPEGOAT

Once again, this is not a historical scene but shows a rule of law for a ceremony on Yom Kippur, the day of atonement. The high priest (Aaron) must draw lots to choose one out of two goats to be slaughtered as a sacrifice for the sins of the people while the other, symbolically laden with the iniquities of Israel, is sent into the desert as a quarry, so to speak, for the desert demon Azazel (Leviticus 16, 7–10; 16, 21–22). In the same way the people are told to choose between Jesus and Barabbas. Jesus will take away the sin of the world as the Lamb of God, while Barabbas is left to meet his fate at the hands of the infernal powers.

ISAAK'S OPFER

Gott wollte Abrahams Glauben und Gehorsam prüfen, indem er ihm befahl, ihm den einzigen Sohn Isaak, den Träger aller Zukunftsverheißungen, als Opfer zu schlachten. Das Bild zeigt die letzte Phase dieser Prüfung: die Ankunft beider auf dem Berge Morija. Isaak trägt selbst sein Opferholz; die Knechte entdecken in einem Dorngestrüpp einen Widder; ein anderer blickt zum Himmel hinauf, ob von dort kein Engel kommt und dem Schrecklichen im letzten Augenblick Einhalt gebietet (Gen. 22,6 und 9). Gott opfert für uns seinen einzigen Sohn. Dieser schleppt ebenfalls sein Opferholz auf eine Bergeshöhe, den Golgatha, aber kein Engel rettet ihn.

THE SACRIFICE OF ISAAC

God wanted to test Abraham's faith and obedience by ordering him to sacrifice his only son, Isaac, who represents all his hopes for the future. The scene shows the last stage of this test, the arrival of father and son on Mount Moriah. Isaac himself carries the wood for his own sacrifice. The servants discover a ram in a thorn bush. Another servant looks up to heaven to see whether an angel will come to stop the terrible deed at the last moment (Genesis 22, 6 and 9). God sacrifices his only Son for us. Jesus likewise drags the wood for his own sacrifice to the top of a hill, Golgotha, but no angel comes to save him.

16

DIE ERHÖHUNG DER EHERNEN SCHLANGE

Als die Israeliten bei ihrem Zug durch die Wüste von einer Schlangenplage heimgesucht wurden, schrie das Volk zum Herrn. Dieser gebot Moses, eine große Schlange aus Kupfer und Erz zu formen und auf einer Signalstange zu erhöhen; wer zu ihr aufschaute, mußte am Schlangenbiß nicht sterben. Moses, erkenntlich an den Gesetzestafeln und den beiden aus seinem Haupte hervorbrechenden Strahlen, weist das Volk auf die Schlange hin. (Num. 21,9). Dies ist die Urform aller Vorbilder, denn Jesus selbst hat in einem nächtlichen Gespräch mit Nikodemus gesagt: *»Wie Moses in der Wüste die Schlange erhöht hat, muß der Menschensohn erhöht werden, damit jeder, der an ihn glaubt, das ewige Leben habe.«* (Joh. 3,16)

THE RAISING UP OF THE BRAZEN SERPENT

On their way through the desert the Israelites were afflicted by a plague of serpents and they cried to the Lord, who told Moses to make a large serpent of copper and bronze and raise it on a pole. Anyone who had been bitten would look at the bronze serpent and be healed. Moses, who can be recognised by the Tables of the Law and the two rays shining from his head, shows the people the serpent (Numbers 21, 9). This is the archetype of all prefiguration scenes because one night, in conversation with Nicodemus, Jesus himself said *"As Moses lifted up the serpent in the desert, so must the Son of man be lifted up, that whoever believes in him may have eternal life"* (John 3, 16).

17

DIE VERHERRLICHUNG CHRISTI

Das Schlußtableau faßt die Erlösungsgeschichte zusammen. Von Adam und Eva geht die Linie über Moses und Johannes den Täufer durch die ausgebreiteten Hände Marias, deren Mittlerrolle durch ihr Knien in der Mitte unterstrichen wird, empor zum auferstandenen und mit der Osterfahne in himmlischer Glorie triumphierenden Heiland. Zu seiner Rechten hält ein Engel das goldglänzende Kreuz, zur Linken ein anderer den Leidenskelch, während Maria Magdalena und die Apostel, die den Beginn ihrer Aussendung durch die Wanderstäbe in ihren Händen bekunden, in Verehrung zu ihm aufblicken.

THE GLORIFICATION OF CHRIST

The final tableau summarises the redemption story. From Adam and Eve the line passes through Moses and John the Baptist, through the outspread hands of Mary, whose role as a mediator is emphasised by her kneeling in the centre, upwards to the risen Christ with the Easter banner, triumphant in heavenly glory. On his right an angel holds the shining gold cross, on his left another holds the cup of suffering, while Mary Magdalene and the apostles, who indicate the beginning of their mission by the staffs in their hands, look up at him in adoration.

Passionstheater mit Dorf (1860)